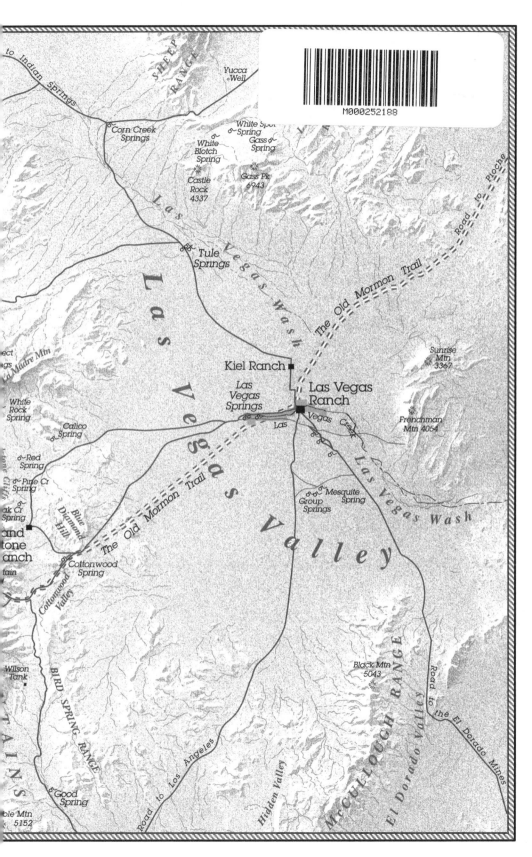

*Helen J. Stewart*

ALSO BY SALLY ZANJANI

*The Unspiked Rail: Memoir of a Nevada Rebel*

*The Ignoble Conspiracy: Radicalism on Trial in Nevada*
(with Guy Louis Rocha)

*Jack Longstreet: Last of the Desert Frontiersmen*

*Goldfield: The Last Gold Rush on the Western Frontier*

*Ghost Dance Winter and Other Tales of the Frontier*

*A Mine of Her Own: Women Prospectors in
the American West, 1850-1950*

*Sarah Winnemucca*

*The Glory Days in Goldfield, Nevada*

*Devils Will Reign: How Nevada Began*

# Helen J. Stewart

## First Lady of Las Vegas

SALLY ZANJANI AND

CARRIE TOWNLEY PORTER

*Stephens Press ❧ Las Vegas, Nevada*

Editor's note: In order to stay true to the spirit and content, the excerpts
from letters and diaries in this book maintain the original spelling and
formatting. Misspellings and variations of punctuation are not typographi-
cal errors, but reflect the times in which they were written.

Publisher: Carolyn Hayes Uber
Editor: Jami Carpenter
Cover and Book Design: Sue Campbell
End Paper Maps: Paul Cirac
Publishing Coordinator: Stacey Fott

First Printing

Cataloging In Publication
Zanjani, Sally; Porter, Carrie Townley.

Helen J. Stewart : first lady of Las Vegas / Sally Zanjani and Carrie
Townley Porter

212 p. : ill., photos ; 23 cm.

ISBN: 1-935043-38-2
ISBN-13: 978-1-935043-38-6

Tells the life story of Helen J. Stewart who moved to Nevada in 1873 with
her husband, was widowed early, and went on to become a successful
rancher and business woman and was the first woman elected to the Clark
County School Board, in addition to many other civic activities.

1. Stewart, Helen J. 2. Nevada—Biography. 3. Women—Nevada—
Biography. I. Title. II. Zanjani, Sally; Porter, Carrie Townley.

[B] dc22 2011 2010942727

STEPHENS PRESS, LLC
A Stephens Media Company

Post Office Box 1600
Las Vegas, NV 89125-1600
www.stephenspress.com

Printed in Hong Kong

*For Keith*

*who was and still is the wind beneath Carrie's wings.*

# Contents

# Acknowledgments

We are greatly indebted to Paul Carson, volunteer at the Nevada State Museum, Las Vegas, who gave us the benefit of his extensive knowledge on Helen J. Stewart and graciously read and commented on the manuscript. Kimberly Higgins provided essential technical help. We are grateful to the members and friends of the Stewart family for sharing their memories with Townley Porter, to Stanley Paher for his expert advice, and to Jill Stovall who generously made sources in her collection available to us.

Colleagues at the libraries, archives, museums, and historical societies where we sought assistance provided much aid and many courtesies. Special mention should be made of Dennis McBride, Nevada State Museum, Las Vegas; Peter Blodgett, Huntington Library; and Su Kim Chung, University of Nevada Las Vegas Libraries, Special Collections. Officials at several county courthouses went far beyond the call of duty in responding to our requests for early records. Carolyn L. Garner-Reagan, at the Huntington Library, undertook helpful research. Cartography was done by Paul Cirac.

# Helen J. Stewart

*and her descendants*

- Archibald Richard Stewart 1834–1884
- **Helen Jane Wiser 1854–1926**
- Frank Royer Stewart 1850–1918

- William James Stewart 1874–1931
  - Lena Carl
  - "Mina" El Mina Hanson 1887–1967
  - Helen Jane Stewart 1914–1956

- Archibald Richard Stewart Jr. 1885–1899

- "Hira"Hiram Richard Stewart 1875–1903
  - Dreeme Gann 1875–1962
  - Leslie Earl Stewart 1898–1983
  - Geneva Stewart 1900–1979

- "Tiza" Flora Eliza Stewart 1879–1955
  - Charles A. Rucker MD
  - Rudolph Anderson
  - Rucker twins 1906–1906

- "Eva" Evaline La Vega Stewart 1882–1947
  - Clarence Arthur Stay 1889–1967
  - James Coffey
  - Clarence Arthur Stay Jr. 1918–1970
  - Evelyn Stay 1923–1986
  - Francis Stewart Stay 1920–1977
  - Clinton Eugene Stay 1926–1986

# Chapter 1: *The Road to Las Vegas*

Helen Jane Stewart resisted moving to the Las Vegas Ranch. In every fiber of her being, she rejected the idea. But Archie, her beloved husband, said they must go, just temporarily. After the previous rancher failed to repay the substantial sum Archie loaned him, Archie had the ranch on his hands, and he insisted that the only way to secure this valuable property was to occupy it. No one else would do it. When one of Archie's partners tried it, he soon gave up. Helen well understood why. The ranch lay in a barren gray desert 170 miles south of the nearest town, Pioche. With the exception of the Indians and a handful of settlers and prowling desperadoes on the run, free to commit any heinous crime in this no man's land, no one lived there. The nearest law officers could only be found in distant Pioche. There would be no one to turn to if outlaws threatened her family.

Nor was there a doctor in the region. Helen and Archie had two young sons and a daughter, and she was four months pregnant. If any of the Stewarts sickened or became seriously injured, she had only the advice and the simple remedies she had obtained from a doctor before leaving. How could she save them in an emergency? And what if something went wrong during the birth of the baby?

Nor was there a school. To Helen's great distress, it had been necessary to withdraw her two boys, Willie and Hira, from primary school after they had barely begun, seriously hampering their education and perhaps their future prospects. Fortunately, her little daughter, Tiza (formally Flora Eliza Jane), was only three, so they should be back in town before she reached school age.

Nor was there a church. The very idea must have seemed ridiculous, out there beyond the edge of the known world. This meant that the devout Episcopalian Helen would be deprived of pastoral guidance and the fellowship of other parishioners in times of acute distress. Nor would there be any of the little pleasures that made life in town enjoyable. No dances, no social events, not even the simple sisterhood of inviting another woman settler for an afternoon cup of tea. No other woman settler lived in the entire valley.

As their wagons, filled with household goods, jolted along the rough dirt road and the dust of their herds rose around them, Helen's apprehension and resistance did not abate. No doubt she consoled herself with the thought that Archie had promised this move would be only temporary. Just a year or two. She had no way of knowing that the Las Vegas Valley would be her permanent home.

Many years later, when civilization finally caught up with Helen, friends found it hard to believe that this petite lady was the quintessential Las Vegas pioneer — widely acknowledged as the First Lady of Las Vegas. Her close friend, Delphine Squires, saw Helen as "a tiny Dresden China piece of femininity with a kindly and gentle disposition; a truly gracious lady with a deep religious nature, seemingly poorly suited for the role she was destined to play." And a leading role it was, for this Dresden china piece of femininity owned and operated a cattle ranch and farm of over a thousand acres, and as a widow with five children, became one of the largest landowners in southern Nevada.[1]

Helen Stewart may have had more adventure in her blood than her friends of later years realized. She came of a westering family. Her father, Hiram Wiser, was born in

1826 in Pennsylvania, descendant of a great grandfather named Hendrik Cridenwiser who had emigrated to New York from the Netherlands. Hiram headed west as a young man and married Delia Gray in Pike County, Illinois when he was twenty-six and she nineteen. Delia gave birth to their eldest daughter, Helen Jane, near Springfield, Illinois on April 16, 1854. Two more girls followed on their Illinois farm, Rachel (named for Hiram's mother and grandmother) in 1856 and Aseneth (named for Hiram's sister) in 1859.[2]

*Helen as a young girl.*
*Nevada State Museum Las Vegas*

Illinois did not hold them over long, because as Helen

later recalled, "my Father like many others was taken with the fever of Westward Ho" and they migrated to Kansas. Hiram and one of Helen's uncles acquired farms there and built two lath and plaster houses on adjoining farms. By 1860 a census taker found the family in Brown County, Kansas, west of St. Joseph, but Hiram would soon be off. The "great Excitement" about gold discoveries at Pikes Peak had erupted, and with it a lucrative opportunity to captain a wagon train bringing the first quartz mill and other supplies to the area. No matter the danger of Indian attack on the Plains. The wagon train had plenty of ammunition and high hopes of finding fortunes in the Rockies. Thrilling stories circulated of riches beyond the dreams of most midwestern farmers gleaned from the gulches in just a few days or weeks. "Pike's Peak or bust" became the slogan for an estimated 100,000 gold rushers, mostly from the Midwest.

They sang:

Oh dear girls now don't you cry,

We are coming back by and by;

Don't you fret nor shed a tear,

But patiently, wait about one year.

Two of Helen's uncles traveled with Hiram, and one of her aunts stayed with Delia, once again alone when Hiram made a second trip the following year. Two of Delia's sisters and their families had settled in the area, though not in hollering distance from the Wiser farm, at least not too many miles away.[3]

Even with so much family support, Delia faced troubled times in "bleeding Kansas." Both in Congress and on its rolling plains, Kansas had become the battleground between North and South as the Civil War loomed on the horizon. In 1856 the "border ruffians," advocates of slavery from Missouri, had sacked the free state capital of Lawrence; in revenge, the half-mad abolitionist John Brown and his followers had murdered five men in the Pottawatomie Massacre. All told, many Kansans were killed in the conflicts of those years, and property losses exceeded $2,000,000. "We lie down in fear at night, and arise in the morning expecting to see the mob approaching," wrote one Kansas housewife. Even in peaceful times, early Kansas settlers had to contend with the droughts that withered their crops, the buzzing rattlesnakes in paths and woodpiles, the raging winds that whistled around their crude cabins, the cholera that decimated families, and the isolation of life in a thinly-populated land.[4] Helen was only a young child then, dark-haired with full rosebud lips. But she may have learned, without knowing that she learned it, how a strong woman with small children can carry on without a husband.

The Wisers remained unsettled. Helen later remembered that her father made a second trip to Colorado with supplies. Bitten by the prospecting bug, he evidently found enough gold in the Rockies for a substantial nest egg, and he could afford to be generous. Hearing that Kansas was drought stricken and some had died of starvation, he brought home from the Plains a great deal of dried venison and buffalo meat, which he divided to relieve the hunger of "our less fortunate neighbors." He moved the thoroughbred stock he had purchased into comfortable quarters in Missouri, where he remained for the winter. Delia and the children started to Iowa with a friend, Dr. Betts, through snow so deep that they were forced to abandon their carriage for a sleigh and cross the ice-bound Missouri River at a small patch of open water. They wintered at the home of Hiram's aunt, joined by Hiram in the spring. An attempt to return to their home in Kansas failed because, as Helen put it, after John Brown's raid at Harper's Ferry, "the War Dogs were soon let loose." Finding the "Times too troublesome," they returned to Iowa, where the twins, Flora and Henry were born in 1863. (Henry died as a child after 1870.) With the Civil War in progress, Hiram and one of Helen's uncles worked in the commissary department in Omaha, while Delia and the children stayed with an aunt and her family in nearby Peru. Although Hiram had new ambitions, he did not sell the Kansas farm for several years.[5]

*Delia Wiser.*
***Nevada Historical Society***

Remarkably, in the same year that the twins were born

— 1863 — the family set off for the West on the California Trail in a small wagon train captained by Dr. Perry. St. Joseph, Missouri, the common jumping-off point for the California and Oregon trails, lay east of Brown County across the Missouri River, and if the excitement was less intense than in the days when many thousands took the trail, it had not abated entirely. America was still on the move. Helen remembered the journey as one of "much danger and hardship."[6] For Delia, the hardship must have been considerable, with two infants only a few months old at her breast and three small children to care for. With such an intrepid pioneer mother beside her, Helen could hardly be less.

Helen would have been primarily concerned with the common responsibility of an eldest daughter, helping her mother care for the younger children. More responsibility than ever rested upon her when several members of the party, including Hiram and Delia, sickened with the scourge of the early Colorado mining camps, mountain fever (possibly a variant form of typhoid). Until their parents recovered, the thought of orphanhood in a far land must have badly frightened the children.[7]

Most emmigrants saw the ensuing journey through the Nevada deserts as an ordeal of thirst, dust, barren sun-baked hills, and dreary gray plains, punctuated by the bleaching skeletons of dead animals. Hiram, ever a prospector at heart, may have looked with a certain longing at the Nevada mountain ranges. In one of them the mighty Comstock Lode had been discovered in 1859, setting off the boom that catapulted a scantily-populated desert to territorial status in 1861, followed just three years later by statehood. Lesser bonanzas had been found since the

Comstock. And (who knew?) there might be more just waiting for a man with a pick. The Wisers' journey was interrupted at Fort Churchill, an adobe compound recently constructed in the desert southeast of the Comstock and the Carson River. The Pyramid Lake War of 1860 had been a disaster for all concerned: first for the volunteers who charged forth under the slogan "an Indian for breakfast and a pony to ride" and suffered heavy casualties when they encountered unexpected resistance from the Northern Paiutes; later, a disaster for the Indians, driven from their Pyramid Lake homeland to the barren deserts of northern Nevada. This conflict demonstrated the necessity to keep a military force nearby and led to the establishment of the fort where the Wisers stopped.

At Churchill two of the Wiser horses caught a fever that proved fatal.[8] Unable to cross the Sierra without a full team, the Wisers lingered farther along the trail in the Carson Valley, a lush meadow land on the eastern edge of the Sierra, where the busy town of Genoa (earlier called Mormon Station) clung to the base of the steep mountains rising straight toward heaven from the valley floor and darkening its homes with shadow by midafter-noon. Celebrated as the first permanent settlement in the future state of Nevada, Genoa showed how young and raw Nevada remained. This site, dating from 1851, was only three years older than the nine-year-old Helen. Many years later when a society of Nevada pioneers was forming, Helen decided that this interlude had been long enough for her to call herself a Nevada pioneer.

The Comstock boom enabled them to continue to California. Helen explained: "Teamsters with twenty Mule teams were buisy hauling over the Heavy Graded

Roads across the Siera Nevada Mountains leading from Sacramento, California to the Fabously Rich Mines great quantities of all kinds of supplies; As they returned empty they generously took the weary Emigrant and his worn out Horses or Oxen as it might be, over the Mountains into that land of peace and plenty; Wevestaid sometime in Carson Valley before availing ourselves of the kindly offer of a gentleman from Placerville, california, who kindly placed our wagon back of his and cared for the two remaining horses." Helen saw the kindly gentleman from Placerville with the twenty mule team as an instrument of divine intervention, "the Good Lord was good."[9]

For the Wisers, the end of the trail came in the autumn of 1863 at Galt, a small farming community in the fertile lands about twenty-seven miles south of Sacramento, California's second largest city in 1860 with 14,000 people. The farmers of Galt had ready access to markets for their produce in addition to the commercial and transport center of Sacramento. Galt was situated a short distance east of the Sacramento River, within easy reach of the metropolis of San Francisco, twenty-five miles north of Stockton, and some thirty-five miles west of the towns of the gold country. Although the exuberant early days of California mining had become in the phrase of historian Rodman Paul "as stable as the grocery business," many among the nomadic tribe of miners had drifted back when Nevada's Comstock faltered in the mid-sixties. Their return gave a new boost to the California economy.[10]

At Galt the Wisers had arrived, in more than one sense of the word. Not only had they reached their destination, the golden land, so different from the ice and snow of the Midwest, but also they had money. They stayed with friends their parents had known in the Midwest until Hiram rented a nearby farm, followed by the purchase of their own place. Whatever the source of their nest egg — possibly gold gleaned from the gulches of the Rockies — the Wisers were not modest in spending it. They bought a handsome house, built in Maine, shipped around the Horn and reassembled, considered so remarkable that it was pictured in an early California history.

Helen attended her first California school, the Sunday school run by the Christian Church, and endured a fright that apparently overshadowed anything she had experienced on the trail. The Sunday sermons of preacher McCarty bore no resemblance to the teachings on the good Lord that Helen had received as a small child at her grandmother's knee. McCarty proclaimed: "That the World was soon coming to an End. That there would be two women standing by the Mill one would be taken one would be left ... There would be Famine and Pestilence and War; I lived in fear of this for many years and during a Heavy Earthquake or two in California I was sure the time was then." None too soon Helen's parents instead sent her to the Presbyterian school, Sunday school, and church.[11]

As Helen grew into a proper young lady in California's increasingly Victorian moral and ethical environment, her family probably encouraged her to take advantage of the cultural opportunities at hand. As a young teenager in 1867-1868, she attended Hesperian College in Woodland, northwest of Sacramento. Although most women did not attend college in those days, middle class families in California were beginning to send their daughters to female seminaries or colleges for purposes of protecting them from undesirable associations and preparing them to make good marriages. Since Hesperian College lacked dormitory facilities, Helen boarded with the family of one of the professors, another Christian Church minister. Obliged to drop out in her first term by a severe attack of lung fever, she continued to board with the doctor who had cared for her and developed a good deal of independence while living apart from her parents at only thirteen.

In the more mature California, so different from the early days in the smaller mining camps when a drunken bacchanal was the principal amusement, literary societies, lyceums, glee clubs, debating societies, and the like emerged. Galt and Hesperian College no doubt kept pace. Despite the strict rules governing conduct at Hesperian ("No student shall be permitted to keep the company of any one of the opposite sex without previous permission of some one of the Teachers ... Any student wishing to attend social parties must obtain permission from some one of the Teachers"), it is likely that the sociable young Helen took advantage of these opportunities for amusement. Likely, too, that her attendance at a coed college and her activities brought her in contact with some young men — possibly young men of whom her parents did not approve, as their insistence that she should marry a successful older man suggests.[12]

Worried over Helen's health, Delia wanted her eldest daughter nearer home. After a short time at home attending a Congregational Church school, another change intervened in 1870 resulting from a recurrence of Hiram's old restlessness. The farm at Galt seemed like an ideal place for a man's later years, perhaps with a daughter or two married to prosperous farmers nearby and grandchildren playing at his feet. Although he kept the farm at Galt, Hiram had no wish to rock and whittle on the porch.

In the Sierra west of present Markleeville near Ebbets Pass, the mining activity at Silver Mountain sounded to him like an opportunity, although the excitement that had erupted in 1863 had already slackened. At the peak, over 300 claims had been staked, despite the absence of any substantial amounts of silver ore, and an instant city of surprisingly numerous wooden buildings sprang up. Hiram planned to drive cattle up to graze in the lush mountain meadows for the summer (of course, this would have allowed a little prospecting on the side). Delia would run a hotel for the mining men who would predictably be investigating the site, as they had earlier headed for the Fraser River, the Kern River, and the Comstock. He bought land, a stock range in Pacific Valley, city lots, and even the former courthouse after Markleeville replaced Silver Mountain as the Alpine County seat.

These holdings would be worth a great deal if the excitement revived and worth very little if Silver Mountain entirely fizzled. In short, Hiram was betting that many others were as restless as he. The 1870 census shows that he brought the family, including Helen. How the sixteen-year-old girl felt about being abruptly transplanted to an isolated mining camp already on the skids with few other women and no social or cultural activities can be readily inferred from her swift departure to stay with friends in Stockton and continue her education at institutions that Delia thought offered "good School advantages," first at Washington High School, then at Professor Woodberry's school. Helen soon became a teacher herself.[13]

Be it in Galt, Silver Mountain, or Stockton, Helen's

parents had laid down the law for her. Their daughter, in her late teens, with dark hair fashionably styled atop her head, an oval face, deep-set, dark, rather dreamy eyes, and full lips that hinted at sensuality, was a pretty girl who would have turned heads in any setting. And would turn them even more in early California where the ratio of women to men remained unbalanced. It appears that some young men began hanging around Helen and that her parents disapproved of them.

Although concern over a daughter's possible marriage to a ne'er-do-well recurs in many times and places, it was particularly acute in post gold rush California. This was a fluid society, where people moved rapidly up and down the social scale and readily socialized outside any fixed orbit. The financial dimension of marriage assumed greater importance than in recent times because for a widowed woman few opportunities had opened in the workplace, and a widow might face great difficulty in supporting herself. Moreover, horror stories abounded in the press and by word of mouth: young widows, poorly provided for, who sank into poverty and ended as prostitutes or suicides; healthy young wives who died mysteriously, perhaps murdered for their money by impecunious husbands; gently raised young women dragged down the road to ruin by alcoholic husbands.[14]

Hiram and Delia wanted to protect their daughters from any such nightmare scenarios. According to family tradition, they insisted that Helen must marry a successful older man. Helen had hardly started teaching when she met a man who satisfied these parental requirements, being twenty years her senior and only six years younger than her father. Dublin born of Scottish ancestry, Archibald Stewart was the operator of several successful businesses near Pioche, Nevada, where his wood ranch provided timber to the area, and his cattle ranged over the sagebrush. Stewart satisfied the Wisers' financial requirements. He also satisfied Helen's own requirements. He was tall and handsome, with curly brown hair, a slightly grizzled short beard and mustache, and intent brown eyes. Indeed, he seems to have swept her off her feet; "Schools and Educational ideas were all cast aside," Helen later wrote. She assented to his proposal, and on April 6, 1873, a few days before her nineteenth birthday she married him in Stockton, at the home of friends, Laura and Andrew Blossom. Because neither signed the marriage documents, Hiram and Delia may still have been at Silver Mountain. However, Hiram had lost his bet and this, their last venture together, would soon collapse.[15]

Helen's honeymoon journey to the "land of the wonderful future," as she called the Nevada desert, seems to have occurred in a golden haze of happiness. From the Palisade stop on the Central Pacific Railroad, they traveled 300 miles south to Pioche in a closed stage coach drawn by six horses, with seating inside and five passengers on top, in addition to the driver, and "all the Baggage that could possibly be crowded on." Fresh horses were provided at intervals, then, "The driver whirled his long lashed whip in air striking the leaders and away we went again." Charles Sumner's account of the same journey a month before Helen suggests some likely details. They would have passed a two-hundred foot cliff where owls roosted and hooted ominously; breakfast at Mineral Hill, consisting primarily of stale soda crackers and a "decoction of chicory and seaweed" that passed for coffee, probably had not improved since Sumner's passage. Helen and Archie paused for a few days to visit friends in rapidly declining Hamilton and in White River.

*Archibald Stewart.*
*Nevada State Museum Las Vegas*

Resuming their places in the "wonderful" stage coach, they finally arrived at the "Mecca of our Dreams" — booming Pioche. The camp was passing through accelerated stages of birth (1870), boom (1871-73), and early decline (1874-75). Brief as it was, Pioche's five-year life span from boom to decay conformed to a common pattern in western mining camps, where disillusion followed hard on the heels of inflated hopes, and few mining excitements became steady long-term producers. Helen saw the last of the boom years when "money and men were plenty" in this "treasure camp of the West." Her pleasure and excitement were palpable. "We found the streets so crowded as to be almost impassible with Fortune seekers … From the Reastuarants to the Court House were such crowds as to makeones progress very slow." Friends of Archie's entertained them for a few days while they bought their stove and furniture. Then they left for Archie's place, Pony Springs, thirty miles north of Pioche in Lake Valley.[16]

*Helen Stewart as a bride.*
*Nevada State Museum Las Vegas*

Though named for a small lake at its northern end, Lake Valley was less a valley than a high desert meadow, dotted with an occasional sagebrush or rabbit brush, rimmed by mountain ranges to the east and west. At Helen's arrival, snow would still have topped the highest cloud-catching peaks, Mt. Wilson at more than 9,000 feet, Dutch John, Parsnip, and Rosencrans, nearly as high. Grasses grew tall and thick in the meadow, basin wild rye and inland salt grass, with waving florets, faintly yellow shading to pink in a certain light. These gave feed for the foraging cattle, Archie's and those of other ranchers that roamed the open range. Deer trails criss-crossed the meadow; quail hastened through the grass; black birds flew overhead. In this vast plain, Pony Springs was not a town, nor even a settlement — just a speck on the map where a spring welled up and a few cottonwoods and cedars grew. For Helen and Archie, it must have been much like being marooned on a desert island, alone together.

The seasons passed at Pony Springs: spring, colored by blossoming wildflowers; summer, when grass greened the lower slopes of the mountains, brooks trickled down, and tall timber at the summits offered deep shade; autumn, silvered with frosty mornings and shortened days, presaging the winter soon to come when fierce north winds raked the valley, bone-chilling cold set in, and the two of them were secluded in the snow. Archie had largely eliminated the teaming side of his business for dealing in cattle and would buy the Tom Knapper Ranch in a few years time. A promising base for his stock, it lay to the west on the Eureka-Pioche stage road. Archie made few poor business decisions, but he may not have realized how living at Pony Springs would affect Helen. She faced the greatest challenge for isolated western pioneer women. Not savage beasts, hostile Indians, or vicious desperadoes, but the loneliness that as New Mexico ranchwoman Agnes

Morley Cleveland has written "called for the last reserve of moral stamina."[17]

In the summer of 1873, Helen became pregnant, and bore their first child, William James Stewart, on March 9, 1874 when she was almost twenty. In a tradition that began in early New England and continued on the frontier, a birth signaled a gathering of the female community; "social childbirth," as historian Laurel Ulrich has termed it. The midwife, relatives, and neighbors would assemble to help, not only at the delivery but during the phase that pioneer women dreaded most, the "lying in" period afterward while the new mother recovered. Isolated at Pony Springs, Helen would have sorely missed the helpful, caring hands of other women. Unless she had gained an Indian helper, Helen may have had only Archie to deliver his child, as many a pioneer husband had done.[18]

Helen had endured enough of isolation. She persuaded Archie to move into town. This meant Pioche, the only settlement within hundreds of miles with a sufficient population to be worthy of the name. Now declining, in 1875 the residents of the entire county did not exceed 2,753, and Pioche may no longer have been "the mecca of our dreams," as Helen had seen it with the rosy glow of a bride. Indeed, it may have been the murder capital of America. The Nevada State Mineralogist reported in 1873: "For a time, Pioche was a scene of lawlessness and horrid murders, which have scarcely ever had a parallel in the history of this coast." Locals took a perverse pride in this reputation. When traveler Charles Sumner arrived on the stage in 1873, the driver announced that of 112 men buried in the public graveyard, only seven had died a natural death. He shamelessly exaggerated. Historian

James Hulse, the leading authority on Pioche, finds forty-six documented homicides, with a few probable additions, but even this figure was hardly negligible in a population shrinking downward from five or six thousand.[19]

Yet the violence did not affect the respectable side of Pioche. Franklin Buck, a resident of Pioche since the earliest days, wrote his family in the East. "About one half of the community are thieves, scoundrels and murderers and then we have some of the best folks in the world … You can go up town and get drunk and get shot very easily if you chose or you can live peaceably." Oddly, the greater the town's prosperity, the more rampant the violence, because it mainly involved "roughs" who gathered to do battle at twenty dollars a day over mining claims. Stone forts were constructed, battles such as the infamous "Washington and Creole War" in 1871 were fought, and the weak town government proved unable to control the violence. What did presently decrease it was the declining value of the mines, which meant they were no longer worth fighting over.[20]

When their wagon rumbled into town, the Stewarts saw some substantial stone buildings on Main Street built in more optimistic days and a conglomeration of wooden shacks huddled in tiers on the slopes of a northeast trending canyon that spread into a broad alluvial fan in Lake Valley. Pioche had burned and been rebuilt in 1871. The streets may have been filthy and cluttered with hogs, both roaming and dead, but it had the churches (Episcopal, Catholic, and, briefly Presbyterian), the friends, and the community activities that Helen had so sorely missed.

As historian Glenda Riley observes, the need for female companionship was a "given fact of life" for pioneer women. Helen exemplified this idea, because with her three sisters and her strong mother at the helm, she had grown up in a community of women. Certainly she longed for female friends when living in the lonely vastnesses of Pony Springs, and in Danish-born Mary Wright Carman, who was to be her dear friend throughout life, she found one. Mary, just a year younger than Helen, had married Sylvester Carman, a blacksmith, shortly before Helen's marriage. They had children almost the same age and saw their little ones christened together in the Episcopal Church. The Stewarts rented a cottage from the Carmans 135 feet east of the substantial brick and stone "million dollar courthouse," notorious for cost over-runs and perpetual mining litigation. At least the Stewarts' new home was in a respectable part of town, where the two young mothers, Helen and Mary, could raise their rapidly growing families in safety, well away from the disreputable dives. In addition to her son Will, Helen and Archie had a second son, Hiram Richard, born in Pioche on November 28, 1875 and soon intimately called Hira, or even Hi. On January 17, 1879, also in Pioche, the Stewarts added a daughter to their growing brood, Flora Eliza Jane, named for Helen's sister Flora and known as Tiza. Mary Carman's infant, Earl Edgar, was a just a day younger than Tiza. Rearing their children together — and comforting Mary after the death of a son in 1880 and her ten-month-old daughter Eveline in 1881 — added to their intimacy.[21]

Consecrated in the palmy days of 1872, the Episcopal Church to which Helen belonged had been built large enough for 250 worshipers, designed in the gothic style, and fitted with pews and other furnishings of California redwood. In early 1875, with his salary shriveling away, the minister decamped and "left us in darkness," as Buck put it. Compelled to make do with the occasional visiting minister, church members endeavored to at least maintain the Sunday school. The darkness would become even blacker when the church building was dismembered in 1897 and went bumping and jolting down the road to be reassembled at Delamar, a newer silver camp to the southwest. There it burned several years later. As town revenues slid downward, maintaining the public school also became a struggle. Valuing her children's education as she did no doubt put Helen in the thick of it. In 1881, her first born son Will (then seven) attended school, soon joined by his six-year-old brother, Hira, in January 1882. The high marks both received in their studies and in deportment must have pleased their parents.

Even though the Stewarts did not arrive until after the peak of the boom, Piochers still enjoyed good times. And not, for respectable citizens, in the 72 saloons, 3 dance halls, and 32 brothels patronized by the roughs in the town's heyday. Since 1873, Pioche had boasted an opera house, Thompson's, which rarely presented an opera but served as a community center. The traditions of Pioche's many Irish, Cornish, and Germans resulted in Christmas celebrations that lasted a week. Archie belonged to the Young Men's Social Club, and the Stewarts attended the club's dances and parties.

Buck described an 1876 New Year's ball, drawing a crowd of over 150 from England, France, and Germany, as well as many large cities in America, so cosmopolitan a gathering that he termed it the "Pacific Coast Style." Men wore kid gloves, women their finest gowns, and Buck approved the polite gentility of the affair. Pioche also had a

CHAPTER 1: THE ROAD TO LAS VEGAS

31

jockey club and a race track four miles from town in the level valley. Everyone, babies and youngsters included, would parade around the track in style, then watch horses from far and wide race for the purse — no small sum as long as the good times lasted. Helen "thoroughly enjoyed living there," Delphine Squires later wrote. "She loved being with people. She enjoyed hearing their footsteps, their voices and their laughter as they passed by her home — things she had missed in those lonely dreary years at Pony Springs. That was an experience she did not care to live over again."[22]

Archie's business dealings during their years in Pioche cannot be readily determined, but he apparently gained a reputation as a tough businessman who drove a hard bargain. It seems cattle remained his primary endeavor, although the price of beef fell drastically as Pioche declined. Buck reported that in the autumn of 1875 it had dropped by more than half, from nine cents per pound in 1872 to four cents. Nonetheless, Archie opened a butcher shop in 1877 that only lasted until he broke up with his partner in a legal dispute. Notably, he had lived around the mining booms for years, yet there is no evidence that he prospected or invested in the mines. His 1878 citizenship papers do not reveal when he came to America. The story that he arrived in the Gold Rush years, while not impossible, would have brought him to California in his teens. Whenever he came, he may have realized early that the most reliable way to succeed was not by mining but by making money from the miners.[23]

Certainly the rapid downfall of Pioche demonstrated the risks of mining. After 1872, speedy extraction exhausted the high grade ore bodies at Pioche's Raymond-Ely Mine,

HELEN J. STEWART: FIRST LADY OF LAS VEGAS

producer of 60 percent of Lincoln County's mineral production, and as the mining companies dug deeper, water flooded the lower levels. There were more difficulties. The demonetization of silver by Congress in 1873 decreased the value of the remaining ore at the same time that multitudinous lawsuits over the mines exhausted the energies and resources of the owners. In 1877-79, a brief boomlet at Jackrabbit and Bristol north of Pioche brightened prospects. Archie appeared on the Bristol voter registration list in that year. This may have meant he did business in Bristol while it lasted or merely signified that his presence at the Knapper Ranch placed him within the Bristol precinct for the moment. Although in 1878 Buck reported on Pioche, "This town has completely gone in. Petered out. Everybody is leaving who can," and departed the following spring, Archie and Helen stayed on — and Archie still had considerable resources at his disposal. In 1879, he made a substantial loan to Octavius Gass, a rancher in the Las Vegas Valley. While capable at prospecting and ranching, Gass was a poor businessman, with a tendency to be overly optimistic on his prospects.[24] Archie's loan would prove to be a fateful decision.

## Chapter 2: *Another Place, Another Life*

In the 1870s Octavius Decatur Gass appeared to be the lord of all he surveyed. That meant a handful of white settlers (five voters, to be exact, in the Las Vegas precinct in 1870), about two hundred Southern Paiutes, and a great deal of desert. Born in Ohio in 1829, he had caught the gold fever and traveled to California by the long ocean voyage around Cape Horn in 1849. Although unsuccessful at mining in the California gold country, he had not abandoned his hopes, and in 1862 he was once again staking claims, mining, and dreaming in El Dorado Canyon forty miles south of Las Vegas on the Colorado River. Legends held that for over a century Indians, Spanish explorers, and a few Mormons had mined at the site. More recently, while it was still part of Arizona Territory, it became a haven for outlaws and deserters from the Civil War. Yet, throughout its long mining history, El Dorado never blossomed into a full scale boom nor ever entirely died. Gass, like many another, failed to find his fortune there.[1]

When mining once more disappointed him, his eyes turned to the Las Vegas Valley, where an early Mormon colony had failed. With undiminished optimism, he believed that he would be different. In 1865 he took over the abandoned Mormon Fort beside the springs on the Mormon Trail, formerly the western part of the Old Spanish Trail. The old trail had served as an important connection between Santa Fe and Los Angeles in the 1830s and 1840s when pack trains struggled through its many difficulties to trade New Mexican woolen blankets for California horses and mules. This caravan trade had ceased in 1848,

supplanted by new roads through southern New Mexico and Arizona created during the Mexican-American War.

Almost immediately the California Gold Rush and Brigham Young's plan to connect Salt Lake City with the Pacific Coast revived this section of the trail. A recent authority, Edward Lyman, points out that the "primary motivation" for establishing Mormon colonies at San Bernardino and San Diego had originally been the need for a link between Brigham Young's inland empire and the world outside to provide passage for manufactured goods needed in Mormondom and arriving converts. Lyman estimates that 5,000 people traveled this route during its first three years as the Mormon Trail. Despite the favorable location of Las Vegas as a stopping place for travelers, intense summer heat, poor crops in the alkaline soil, quarrels, and thefts by Indians less than enthusiastic about converting to the Mormon faith, had finished the earlier Mormon colony. Gass withstood the heat, frequently announced good crops, and even learned to speak Southern Paiute, but he considered the Indians "a great pest and nuisance."

Photos of Gass fail to convey the taste for adventure, the resourcefulness, or the leadership qualities that he evidently possessed. Gray-eyed, with a curly brown beard, he stood six feet tall; the Indians called him "long back" for his unusually broad shoulders. Probably facing little electoral competition from the few settlers within riding distance, he represented the area in the Arizona legislature from 1865 until 1868 during the transitional period when the government was transferring it from Arizona to the new state of Nevada. To avoid Indian troubles in Arizona, he and a friend traveled three hundred miles by rowboat down the Colorado River, whirling through the rapids of

Black Canyon, and on to Yuma, where they continued by stage to the legislative session at Tucson.[2]

Gass made shorter trips as well, regular runs to sell beef and produce to the miners in El Dorado Canyon, and occasional visits to Pioche. Beginning in 1871, he also began making frequent sixty-mile trips to the Mormon settlements established in the 1860s in the Moapa Valley, St. Thomas, St. Joseph, West Point, and Overton. Originally planned as way stations for the Colorado River trade, these settlements became agricultural communities after the river trade proved impractical. The reason for Gass's sudden interest in the Moapa Valley was a brave and pretty black-haired woman, Mary Virginia Simpson, living on a farm with her sister's family. They married in Pioche in 1872 and had seven children, two of whom died in infancy at the Las Vegas Ranch.

During his courtship of Mary, Gass regularly crossed the fifty-five mile desert, probably more dangerous than the dreaded Forty Mile Desert on the California Trail farther north. Fortunately, he had no need to cross the quicksands of the Virgin River north of the Muddy Valley settlements. This was an arduous process sometimes involving thirty-two crossings to avoid the fate of a heavy wagon that sank out of sight in the sands. According to Lyman, the western section of the Mormon Trail from Beaver Dam to Baker, encompassing Las Vegas, was "the most difficult stretch of wagon road used regularly by pioneers or freighters anywhere in the continental United States" (although disagreement might have been expressed by gold rushers struggling on the trails farther north). Undoubtedly, the southern desert held perils for novices. Gass offered advice to unwary desert travelers he had no wish to bury: never travel alone; feed your animals and rest before starting; gorge yourself with water and bring a full canteen; never leave the trail; and never "play with the Indians, like some rattle-brained boy."[3]

Although the desert certainly posed the greatest dangers, historians Ralph J. Roske and Michael S. Green have found that the Southern Paiutes "occasionally attacked" the ranch. In one often-recounted 1878 episode, an Indian runner warned that Indians from across the river (possibly Mojaves) would attack. The Gass family, all the children suffering with whooping cough, fled in an improvised covered wagon through a violent rainstorm lasting all night to take refuge with miner C.A. Bidwell and his wife at Ivanpah. They later returned to find everything peaceful at the ranch under the control of the friendly Chief Tecopa. On another occasion, local Indians led by a renegade half-breed took the offensive. Gass stacked all his guns on the dining room table and allowed the Indians to see them. As his Chinese cook rang the triangle gong, Gass warned them that men would be coming to man those guns. The intrepid Mary Gass then seized a gun from one of the hostile Indians and aimed it at his face. The matter ended amicably, with Gass and the chief smoking a peace pipe — a large meerschaum belonging to Gass.[4]

It is doubtful that attacks discouraged Gass, but during his fifteen years at the Las Vegas Ranch, he had shown a certain ambivalence about it. On the one hand, he developed and expanded it, also purchasing the adjacent Spring Ranch. He added this to the original ranch and acquired 640 acres from the U.S. government under the Desert Lands Act; he now owned all the water in the valley, an indication of plans for the future. On the other hand, he

HELEN J. STEWART: FIRST LADY OF LAS VEGAS

made sporadic attempts to unload the ranch. He first offered it for sale divided into parcels in 1868, then changed his mind. In the midst of financial troubles that put the ranch on the delinquent tax list in 1873, Gass secured an extension and mortgaged it to William Knapp in 1876 for $3,000, which Gass repaid. Ever too sanguine about his prospects, Gass plunged more deeply into debt three years later. Moreover, his unwise involvement in litigation against the wealthy Abel Stearns over tin mines exacerbated his need for money. In 1879, he sought and received a $5,000 loan from Archie Stewart, a loan tantamount to a sale because he could never repay it at the extortionate rate of two and a half percent interest a month that Archie charged. This high interest rate showed the cold calculating business methods that earned Archie the enmity of many in Pioche. Gass expressed concern about schools for his children and began seriously looking at small farms in California. In the summer of 1880, when he predictably defaulted, Gass deeded all his rights in the ranch to Archie, unless he could repay within nine months — an impossibility. After briefly running the ranch until Archie took over, the Gass family moved to a small farm near Pomona.[5]

Archie's original plan envisioned using the Las Vegas Ranch to raise horses, cattle, and other stock as well as crops. To this end, he entered into partnership with two Pioche merchants, George Hagerty and George Barton, anticipating a freighting business and a store that would sell liquor and provisions at Pioche. Under their agreement, Archie contributed the lion's share ($9,635, all but $4,000 represented by the Las Vegas Ranch), while Hagerty and Barton each put in $5,761. Hagerty moved south to manage the ranch. He apparently did well, curing a ton of raisins, making 600 gallons of wine, and establishing a store for travelers, but by the spring of 1882, he had had enough of life in the Las Vegas Valley. On March 1, 1882, the partnership legally dissolved, and Archie received the ranch with all livestock and appurtenances.

It had obvious disadvantages. Only four years had passed since an Indian attack sent the Gass family fleeing through the night. Although from 1855 to 1868 the trail had been "one of the busiest freight routes in the West," the traffic passing through the ranch was now light, mostly Mormons traveling between Utah and San Bernardino. The completion of the Central Pacific and Union Pacific railroads in 1869 provided an easier and faster means to move freight and travelers from east to west, and the freight traffic passing through Las Vegas dwindled. Moreover, mining at El Dorado had slackened. Pioche was 170 miles to the northeast. Archie, however, was not the man to write off a valuable ranch, even though it had defeated all those who attempted to operate it: the Mormons, the resourceful Gass, and most recently, Hagerty.[6]

Archie decided that the best way to save his investment in the Las Vegas Ranch would be to move there with his family for a year. Just a year, he told Helen. Living in another remote place, even more distant from any town than Pony Springs, deeply concerned Helen, and she tried to dissuade him. To no avail. Even though Helen expected another baby in September, even though they had three small children, eight-year-old Will, six-year-old Hira, and little three-year-old Tiza, and they would need to take the boys out of school, Archie remained adamant. Knowing that her family would be alone in the distant desert, far from medical help, Helen undertook a grim task and consulted a doctor before leaving. He gave her some simple medical supplies and advice for emergencies: in the case of a severed artery, she should apply a tourniquet above the wound and try to tie the severed ends; spider webs should be applied to a severed vein until the flowing blood congealed. Helen would do well in the unaccustomed role of home physician, through additional childbirth and ordinary illnesses. So far as is known, she never needed the doctor's advice on severed arteries and veins. All those in her family would either be healthy or past all human help. In April 1882, their cavalcade set off from Pioche on a most unpleasant journey loaded with household goods and farming implements. The wagons jolted over the bumps of a road that was exceedingly rough, even by the standards of remote desert roads in the 1880s. Dust rose from the herds of cattle and horses they drove before them. Helen could have borne the jolting and the dust with a better heart had it not been for her misery at making this journey into isolation and loneliness. It would be Pony Springs all over again — only worse.[7]

Despite her apprehensions, Helen would have seen the Las Vegas Ranch in a pleasant guise before the heat of summer locked in. The main ranch house that was to be her future home — temporarily, just temporarily, Archie had promised her — had thick adobe walls. A bedroom, kitchen, and living area comprised the house. Two bedrooms were added later, connected to the kitchen. Storage buildings and a blacksmith shop stood nearby, and rock fences surrounded a square and treeless stockade where horses and some cattle were driven at night. A willow break lay east of the stockade, with fields of alfalfa, grain, and corn beyond. As we know from historian Stanley W.

Paher's research, the fields yielded two crops annually: first, the grains, such as wheat and barley, harvested in late spring by Indian women with winnowing baskets; then vegetables, including corn, melons, and especially pink Mexican beans, an important food source for the Indians, supplementing the mesquite beans from wild bushes growing plentifully on the nearby flats. Since the time of the Mormon colonists, the fields had been fenced with thorny mesquite bushes, the upper branches of which kept even the jack rabbits at bay. South of the willow break, fruit orchards of oranges, lemons, peaches, apples, apricots, figs, and even pomegranates had been planted. The Big Spring, a large, smooth pond with lukewarm water boiling up in the depths beneath, flowed into the Las Vegas Creek and watered the ranch.

As the Stewart wagon rolled into the stockade, the springtime promise of leafy green trees and thriving crops may not have appeared wholly displeasing to Helen. Not one to recline with the vapors, despite her condition and the summer heat, Helen soon threw herself with a will into her new role as mistress of the oasis on the southern desert trail where the Mormon Trail from Salt Lake City brought travelers headed to or from southern California. Mary Gass had employed a Chinese cook. Helen did the cooking herself, aided by Southern Paiute women, who soon became not merely hired help, but friends. Helen, devout Episcopalian though she was, had none of the racist ethnocentric attitudes sometimes shown by white women missionaries in the West.[8]

If Helen feared Indians as a result of her father's perilous passages across the Plains to and from Pike's Peak or shared the anxieties commonly felt by travelers on the

*During Helen's years in the Las Vegas Valley, Southern Paiute women like this one worked for her and became her friends. UNLV Special Collections*

California Trail, any negative feelings soon melted when she became acquainted with the Southern Paiutes. Seeing them bereft of their traditional lands and food sources, she sympathized with their plight and tried to help sustain them. She nursed them when they sickened. She admired the adaption to a harsh land that had brought them so close to nature. Their legends and their artwork in basketry charmed her. The ritual aspect of their beliefs, she came to think, brought them close to God. On the death of Nipe, an Indian girl she was especially fond of, Helen would one day accord Nipe the honor of burial in the Stewarts' small family graveyard. Helen's attitude of acceptance and friendship differed markedly from Gass, who thought the Southern Paiutes "a great pest and nuisance," and the Indians knew the difference. No more "occasional attacks" on the Las Vegas Ranch occurred after the Stewarts took charge.[9]

Often Helen had many to cook for with her large and growing family, the hired hands, and five or more travelers on the trail. She never knew in advance how many she would need to provide with a meal. Later she said that when she saw the dust from the wagons of approaching travelers from the north she fired up the wood stove, put on the coffee, started potatoes and vegetables cooking, prepared biscuits, and finally rang the dinner bell. Parties driving from the south came without warning, and at times the family awoke in the morning to see wagons that had arrived in the night.

As well as purchasing meals, the travelers often wanted to buy various supplies from foodstuffs to red underwear, to take care of blacksmithing and other repairs, and to drive their wagons into the creek so the waters would moisten the desert-parched wood. Helen graciously made them welcome. Although the dances and community activities and her close friendship with Mary Carman at Pioche were lost to her, she enjoyed visiting with the women travelers. In Squires' words: "No one ever passed her door but was cordially welcomed, cheered and helped, mentally, morally, and by this ministering angel."

Helen took particular pleasure in their company because

no ranch women settlers lived in the Las Vegas Valley. The C.W. Farrell Ranch was a long ride to the northwest at Indian Springs. Mrs. Joseph Yount had lived at the Manse Ranch in the Pahrump Valley since 1876 when Indians under "Horseshoe Em" killed her family's horses, forcing them to halt on their journey from Oregon to Arizona. The formidable Mrs. Yount sounds well worth knowing, and when Helen became acquainted with her, the two families established a tradition of trading holidays. The Stewarts spent the Fourth of July at the Manse Ranch and entertained the Younts during Christmas at the Las Vegas Ranch. Nonetheless, Helen could hardly pay an afternoon call on Mrs. Yount because the Manse Ranch lay sixty miles away to the southwest over the Charleston Range and far away, and the Moapa Valley settlement across the desert to the northeast was just as far in the opposite direction.[10]

In the Las Vegas Valley, the only other settlers were George Allen at a coal camp ten miles to the south and two others who would figure importantly in Helen's life. The first was James Bernard Wilson, born in 1828, youngest of ten children in a large Ohio family. He became a forty-niner, and in 1850 the California census taker found him mining in Rough and Ready, a small mining camp of 672 men and no women east of Nevada City. In 1863, he joined the California volunteers, Company 1 of the Fourth Infantry Regiment, stationed at Fort Mohave, Arizona Territory, to counter the Confederate drive in the southwest during the Civil War. Because the California volunteers were mostly miners, they overlooked nothing when scouting and thoroughly prospected Mohave County and El Dorado Canyon. After leaving the army with the rank of sergeant, Wilson began buying land in Lincoln County, but mining fever still coursed in his blood. In 1871, with various partners, he located mining claims in the Bristol district near Pioche. The last of these, which they named the "Poor Man's Lode," suggests that they had not been overly successful. Within the next four years, Wilson profited from the sale of his last mining claim, the "Sweepstakes" in the Paharanagat Lake mining district, located the Spring Mountain Ranch in the Las Vegas Valley with partner John Howell, sold it to Mary Gass, and abandoned mining for stock raising. Another spot nestled against the Spring Mountains had caught his eye, a place of surpassing beauty, with grassy meadows, a spring-fed creek bordered by cottonwood trees that turned golden in fall, and nearby thickets of acacia-mesquite. It served as an alternate route on the trail. Outlaws engaged in Indian slave trading and horse thievery no longer used it as a base as they had done in the 1830s and 1840s, but occasional wagons and pack trains still passed through. In 1876 Wilson and a new partner, George Anderson, took possession of the place, which they named Sand Stone Ranch. They raised stock and sold beef and produce to travelers and to El Dorado. They moved hermit crab-like into a stone hut reputedly built by grain traders from Ivanpah, soon replaced by a log house. There they lived with Annie, an Indian woman of unusual charm, the wife of Wilson or Anderson or both, and three half-Indian children, the progeny of Wilson or Anderson or both. In 1882, Jim Wilson was fifty-four, long-nosed, thin-lipped, bearded, wary-eyed, with the lean, hard-bitten face of a frontiersman. But the heart within was kind and full of admiration for Helen Stewart.[11]

*Jim Wilson*
*UNLV Special Collections*

The other denizen of the Las Vegas Valley who would figure in Helen's future was Conrad Kiel, a venerable man of seventy-six, a small rancher and sawmill operator, living with his grown son Ed a mile and-a-half northwest of the Stewarts. He had other children but they had not accompanied him west, nor had his wife. Kiel must have been a source of unease to the Stewarts because of the company he kept. His place was a haven for outlaws, including the notorious desperado Hank Parish.

Born in Nova Scotia in 1840, Parish had lived and raised a family in Oregon (so he said) before what the press termed his "bloody career" in southern Nevada began. And a bloody career it was. He first appears on the census in 1880 in El Dorado, where his early killings took place and his vindictive nature became evident. His first victim was a man named Taylor in 1879. He shot two more men, N. Clark and James Greenwood, over a card game, and temporarily made himself scarce. Paher observes that Parish was not arrested because the county commissioners decided they could not afford the expense of trying him. Returning to find Greenwood still clinging to life and awaiting transport for medical treatment, Parish declared he would finish the job and kill Greenwood. A friend of Greenwood's averted this by paying Parish the $100 he claimed Greenwood owed him in the card game. Before the law belatedly caught up with Parish in 1890, he admitted killing three men and shooting three others whom he evidently did not count. The causes that roused him to murderous rage appear slight: the card game with Greenwood and Clark; the knifing of miner A.G. Thompson who the drunken Parish erroneously believed had laughed at him; and the Royal City murder that finally sent him to the gallows in 1890.[12]

Undoubtedly the fact that law enforcement did not exist in the Las Vegas Valley sharpened the Stewarts' apprehensions. Tacitly acknowledging that the vast area covered by their counties exceeded their policing capacities, lawmen in both Lincoln and neighboring Nye counties essentially left the settlers in the southern region to fend for themselves in a kind of "no man's land." The coroner might hold the formality of an inquest, as when the frontiersman Jack Longstreet shot Alexander Dry in the Moapa Valley in 1884; yet typically, the inquest would conclude that without witnesses, no one knew what had happened so no one could be tried. More often no inquest convened in the "southern country," as the region was then known in points farther north. A local resident later said of one of these murderers in Ash Meadows, "They just let him stay around no more than if he was shooting a dog."[13]

If Helen was uneasy, the terse, unemotional entries in her Day Book gave no sign of it, nor did she indicate any awareness of ranch financial matters. Indeed, she knew next to nothing about Archie's business affairs, in keeping with the doctrine of "separate spheres" so prevalent in the latter nineteenth century. She might occasionally pay a ranch worker — or without instructions from Archie, not pay them, as in one instance fraught with consequences — but her sphere was the household. Operating the ranch and related financial matters remained unknown to her.

Yet, ironically, Helen became the closest thing to a banker in the Las Vegas Valley. One day while washing windows she found a loose board above the window. The space behind that board provided the perfect spot to hide money. She also served as the banker for prospectors, concealing their money in baking soda cans. In an age when banks frequently failed, wiping out the savings of depositors, these men knew their money would be safer with Helen than in a bank — as well as a good deal handier.[14]

In June 1882, Archie turned down an $11,000 offer from California buyers that would have brought a profit, nearly doubling his investment after only two months in residence. Clearly he had great faith in the future of the Las Vegas Ranch, and possibly Helen, now in her established place as mistress of the trail oasis, had begun to see the value of his investment, while not accepting the ranch as a desirable place to live. On a trip to Pioche in December to deliver a ton of peaches and raisins, Archie told inquiring friends that she was contented, which may have reflected his hope, not her reality. Life on the ranch would soon become even more difficult for her, and she would need to draw on all the physical strength she possessed. On September 22, 1882, Evaline La Vega, her second daughter, was born. Helen chose the name "Evaline" to honor her friend Mary Carman, who had recently lost a daughter named Evaline; the middle name was an adaption of Las Vegas, the child's birthplace. In addition to her role as hostess of the trail, Helen now had the demanding care of an infant and three young children, ages eight, six, and three.[15]

So far as is known, Archie had plenty of experience as a stockman but not in farming. Nonetheless, he learned quickly, the crops thrived, and he made improvements, putting in a picket fence and introducing alfalfa. Although he occasionally drove wagon loads of produce to Pioche, his main market was the mining camp at El Dorado, where he regularly sent wagons of produce and beef.

And sometimes El Dorado came to the ranch. The purple grapes he grew were a superior variety, developed from cuttings brought from France and Italy by Colorado River ferryman Daniel Bonelli, a Mormon. When Bonelli was on his mission to win converts to the church, he obtained the cuttings, an innovation at odds with the Mormon prohibition against alcoholic beverages. After Archie pressed wine

HELEN J. STEWART: FIRST LADY OF LAS VEGAS

in September, the word spread quickly to the miners. The *Pioche Record* reported: "All quit work for some time and are rusticating up at the Vegas Ranch, having a jolly time drinking wine. Whenever any of them get drunk they are placed in the works of the roots of a tree and made to sit there until sobered." More congenial visitors for Helen than drunks hiccupping in the tree roots had come when Andy Fife brought his ailing wife and his children from the Canyon to spend a part of the summer of 1882 at the ranch. Many travelers came to see the ranch much as Mrs. Fife did, a place of rest and recuperation over which the kind and capable Helen presided.[16]

July 1884 began in an ordinary way, although there was some unpleasantness with a former employee named Schyler Henry who had been saying disparaging things about the Stewarts for about a week. While Archie was away delivering a load of produce at El Dorado Canyon, Henry tried to frighten Helen into paying him, but soon found that despite her petite stature and her lonely situation she was not a woman to be stampeded. Lacking instructions from Archie, she refused his demands. Henry retaliated by retreating to the Kiel Ranch and slandering the Stewarts whenever he could find a listener. He evidently included ugly remarks about Helen's conduct during her husband's absences. Apparently the confrontation with Henry occurred on the eleventh, when Helen also noted that Mr. Moore arrived from Pioche and ranch workers baled hay.

Her Day Book entries around this time seem brief and mundane. On Monday she had been sick all day, for although little Evaline was just a toddler, not yet two-years-old, Helen was three months pregnant with her fifth child, due in the coming winter. She was well enough to scald the beds on Tuesday (possibly to rid them of bedbugs brought by the travelers). The next day she noted that Hank Parish had returned from the Canyon. Valley residents George Allen and Mr. Frazier stopped by on the tenth. On July 13 Archie came home from El Dorado about ten o'clock in the morning. After he had eaten and rested, Helen told him about the upsetting matter with Henry. To avoid alarming her, Archie concealed his fury at the man who had tried to coerce his wife. Whether he knew Hank Parish had returned from El Dorado is not clear, but Parish's presence would not have changed his course — and it was not the course assumed by his wife and oldest son. About two o'clock Will Stewart watched his father saddle his horse and ride toward the cattle range, taking his Henry rifle, a formidable .44 caliber, brass-framed, lever action weapon capable of firing sixteen bullets without reloading. Often Archie rode out with the Henry, but this time he had a purpose that neither Will nor Helen guessed. Neither gave the rifle any thought because Archie headed southward in the direction opposite to the Kiels. Helen assumed he was going to George Allen's coal camp. The next news Helen had of her husband was a terse note from Conrad Kiel:

"Mrs. Sturd Send a Team and take Mr. Sturd away he is dead. C. Kiel."[17]

# Chapter 3: *Widow*

Helen flew to her horse, hastily giving orders to the hired men for the wagon to follow and leaving the children with Mr. Frazier. She "went as fast as a Horse would carry me." It was a day etched forever in her memory. "The man that killed my husband ran as I approached as I got to the corner of the house I said Oh where is he Oh where is he and the Old Man Kiel and Hank Parish said here he is and lifting a blanket showed me the lifeless form of my husband. I knelt beside him took his hands placed my hand upon his heart and looked upon his face."[1]

Archie had suffered four wounds: a bullet hole in his hair about two inches above the temple; a wound just above the left breast, the bullet exiting under the right arm, which Frazier and Allen later concluded had been made by a pistol; a shot in the shoulder, according to Kiel and Parish; and a rifle wound under the right ear, probably inflicted after he fell. His cheekbone and forehead had also been broken by a blow with a heavy instrument. Without doubt, Archie had been ambushed and shot by men wielding more than one gun.[2]

The extreme summer heat in the Las Vegas Valley and the long distance from a coroner necessitated a hasty burial of Archibald Stewart the day after he died, but Helen would not have him laid unceremoniously in the ground, even though there was no planed lumber at the ranch. She would see that he had a proper burial, if she had to order the outer doors ripped from the ranch house to do it. His coffin, constructed by George Allen from these doors, was not a simple rectangle but wider at the top to accommodate his broad shoulders and narrowing toward the feet. Standing over her husband's coffin, surrounded by her children, her employees, George Allen, Mr. Frazier and some Indian friends, Helen began the funeral service. With trembling hands, holding the small prayer book, she read: "I am the resurrection and the life saith the Lord: he that believeth in me, though he were dead, yet shall he live: and whosever livith and believeth in me, shall never die." Hearing these words, the grief and fear the children undoubtedly felt over the murder of their father can well be imagined, and one may already have started to nurse a vision of revenge. Although Helen had sent for Jim Wilson, he did not arrive until the following day. Archibald Stewart was the first of nine to be buried in the hard, pale caliche ground later to become known as the "Four Acres," the amount of land that Helen would always retain for family burials.[3]

Helen had no experience in managing the ranch; that had always been Archie's sphere. Nonetheless, the pressing need to shoulder ranch activities left her no time to mourn or succumb to her fears. She quickly rose to the necessity. A large amount of fruit was ripening rapidly, and on the Saturday after the funeral, Allen took a load of produce to El Dorado for her, beef jerky to be sold at seventy cents a pound, and also corn, wine, and fruit, followed by another trip the next week. Both Allen and Wilson did what they could to help and promised to give her any possible aid when needed, but she realized that she could not ask them to neglect their own affairs for long.[4]

While she carried on with ranch management and the legal necessities that followed Archie's murder, terror raked Helen's heart, because she did not know if the killings had run their course, and she believed the three men at Kiel's capable of anything. Her desperation showed in the letter she wrote to Archie's lawyer in Pioche, George Sawyer, to find out if her husband had made a will. "I write to you in great distress of mind Hoping you as a husband and father will aid me to the best of your ability. I am left all alone here and my little children Fatherless by the hand of a murderer. My beloved husband and only friend was murdered Sunday the 13th at Mr. Kiels one mile and half from here while defending the honor of his family from a black hearted Slanders tongue." Feeling herself defenseless, she expressed the hope: "If I have friends in Pioche I pray they will come and help me." With astonishingly cruel callousness, Parish, the man Helen came to believe was the very devil himself, came to her door six days after Archie's murder and demanded the fifteen dollars owed to Schyler Henry. Too frightened to refuse, Helen paid.

If Archie had not left a will, she instructed Sawyer to take any legal action necessary to ensure her retention of the property and her appointment to administer the estate. The *Pioche Weekly Record* partially quoted a portion of her letter on August 2, 1884. The full version, part of it marked private, has been preserved in her Day Book. Here she avers that more than one person took part in killing Stewart. She expressed fear because she was alone among a gang of cutthroats and murderers and felt it dangerous to "say or do anything as we are overpowered by numbers and still threatened." Allen, Wilson, and Frazier added their signatures to the letter to corroborate her statements.[5]

Helen's evident belief that she could expect no protection from the law was amply borne out. With no great sense of urgency, Deputy Sheriff Sam Smith arrived in the Las Vegas Valley nearly three weeks after the murder, to bring in Henry, Parish, and Kiel to appear before the grand jury and to subpoena Helen. Typically, Parish had vamoosed, and also typically, no effort was made to find him. An unsigned letter in Helen's papers acidly observed, "Three weeks after the killing the Deputy Sheriff a very amiable man arrives at the sciene of the murder and arrests, what remains of the participants ..."[6]

Deputy Smith's laggardly arrival considerably post-dated the news of Stewart's murder. The first report had come to Pioche via the mail rider from the Moapa Valley and ascribed the crime to Parish. A brief note from Helen to D.C. Clark stating that her husband had been murdered came next. Further news reached Pioche in a letter written from the Moapa Indian Reservation on July 17 by J.T. Moore, considered a credible source because he had taught for several years in the Pioche, St. Thomas, and St. Joseph schools. Based solely on what Kiel and Henry told him two days after the murder, Moore related that upon learning that Henry had quit, Stewart had armed himself and approached the Kiel ranch from the north by a circuitous route. He hitched his horse to a tree behind a cluster of grape vines and proceeded on foot. Henry spotted him running in the direction of the door about thirty feet from the house holding his rifle in position to fire. All the windows and doors of the house were open, with weapons standing against each window — apparently preparations for Stewart's arrival. Henry, seated by a south window, saw Stewart and reached for a shotgun standing against the window. Finding it unloaded, he sprang across the room and grabbed from its scabbard a Spencer rifle leaning against the north window. Stewart fired, missing Henry, and prepared to fire again. Henry stepped behind the door, while Stewart fired through the door, grazing Henry's arm. Henry, reloading his rifle, stepped out from behind the door. Both men fired. Henry received a flesh wound in the hip, and Stewart a shot through the chest. No words were spoken during the affray. Both fired again. Stewart, taking a shot in the head, was instantly killed. Moore absolved Conrad and Ed Kiel from any part in the gunfight.[7]

Conrad Kiel's version contended that Henry's abrupt departure from the Stewart Ranch so angered Archie that he went gunning for Henry without further provocation. Nonetheless, it seems unlikely that Archie could be so strongly provoked by the simple resignation of an employee. As Helen's ledgers show, ranch hands stayed for awhile and then moved on. Henry's slanders and harassment of Helen seem a more realistic reason for Archie's sudden decision to confront the man than a simple argument with an employee over wages. This raises the question: did Henry deliberately provoke Archie because the group at Kiel's intended to kill him?[8]

There is some evidence of concerted action. According to Kiel, only Stewart and Henry were involved. Yet the wounds described by Helen, Allen, and Frazier indicate otherwise. The shot in the chest was attributed to a pistol shot, although Henry admitted to using only rifles. Moore's description of the gunplay failed to jibe with Stewart's injuries, which suggest violence after Stewart fell. Did the gratuitous shots to his body after his death indicate revenge? Certainly he bore more wounds than could have occurred in the gunplay between Stewart and Henry described by Moore. Entries in Helen's Day Book show that Parish had returned to the Las Vegas Valley from El

Dorado Canyon four days before Archie was killed. Had Parish taken part in the murder?[9]

In Helen's eyes, then and forever after, he was the one primarily responsible for killing Archie, as is shown in a letter entitled "Adversity of Justice," unsigned and undated but written in Helen's hand in 1884 some time after the murder. Here Helen referred to the "infernal set of men" at Kiel's and traced Archie's murder to the theft of his horses a year and-a-half previously; Stewart, of course, was not a man to let the matter pass. Although he recovered his horses, the thief escaped, and "Stewart's life has been threatened ever since." After Stewart also retrieved a neighbor's stolen cattle, the thief sent word that he would kill Stewart "the first opportunity"; although Stewart notified the authorities, they failed to take action. The result was Stewart's murder, for which Helen blamed Lincoln County officials: "all this time Officials are indifferent to the matters," further observing that had measures been taken "one year ago to surpress these criminals there would not have been so many outlaws in the lower part of the county and one more good honest citizen would be alive."[10]

No unbiased witness had seen Archie's death, but Helen believed she knew what had happened. As she later told Delphine Squires, Helen was convinced that Schyler Henry, Conrad Kiel, and Hank Parish all were involved; Ed Kiel was absent in El Dorado Canyon. All three were enemies of Archie's: Schyler Henry, obviously; Conrad Kiel and Archie had long been hostile to each other; if Parish could shoot two men over a card game, he would do no less for the man who had accused him of horse thievery and tried to bring the law down on his head. Quite possibly the vengeful spirit of each of these men — and especially

HELEN J. STEWART: FIRST LADY OF LAS VEGAS

Parish — emboldened the others and finally goaded them into action.[11]

Helen's parents came to care for the children and the ranch while she went north to Pioche for the trial of her husband's murderers and the settlement of the estate. She traveled in a wagon with Deputy Smith at the reins, and the county charged her half the price of the team. On August 11, Helen entered a building well known to her but one she surely had never expected to see under such circumstances — Lincoln County's infamous million dollar courthouse, a monument to the greed and folly of palmier days. The courthouse's red brick exterior had been a part of the landscape of her life during the years when she lived with Archie and the children in the little house 135 feet to the east, rented from the Carmans during their years in Pioche. Nonetheless, those 135 feet might have been 135 miles, because the courthouse was another world, one of bitter and endless mining litigation and prosecutions for crimes committed in the rough part of town, a world that Helen would never have expected to intersect with hers. Now she must pass through the arched doorway, sedately seat herself on one of the hard wooden benches in the courtroom, watch the summer sun pouring in through the tall windows, and hope for justice against all odds.

The case became the word of Helen against the testimony of Henry and Kiel, the only witnesses present at the shooting other than the absent Parish. It was not the custom in Lincoln County at that time to convict a man for murder without impartial eyewitness testimony. Yet this murder was unusual. More commonly, a saloon brawl ended in a killing; in the words of early historian Myron Angel, "Persons meet in saloons, bagnios and gambling places with deadly weapons upon their persons; they drink, gamble when half intoxicated, banter each other, and at last draw out their weapons and for fancied causes alone slay each other."[12]

*The Pioche Courthouse where Archibald Stewart's murderers were tried in 1884.*
*Stanley W. Paher*

In this case, however, the motive remained hidden. Clearly, Archie had a talent for making enemies, and his business methods earned him no friends. Perhaps his prosperous ranch, his pretty wife, and his fine family aroused envy among the less fortunate. But neither Henry, nor Parish, nor Kiel had gained anything tangible from his death, neither his lands, nor his fortune, nor his wife. On one point Helen never deviated: Parish was the one

HELEN J. STEWART: FIRST LADY OF LAS VEGAS

primarily responsible for her husband's murder. If Henry's claim of self defense is discounted, no motive seems likely beyond satisfying a spirit of revenge. Perhaps the three egged each other on with Parish in the lead, as Helen believed. He was the only known killer among them and the one with the strongest cause for animus against Archie.[13]

Archie's motive is somewhat clouded as well. On July 5, Helen had written an entry in her Day Book so brief that it raises more questions than answers: "G. Allen started to Canon. told of H lying." Archie had not yet left the ranch for El Dorado then, so if "H lying" refers to Henry's slanders, Archie would probably have known about them more than a week before he rode out with his rifle to confront Henry, and Henry, according to Helen's Day Book, did not leave the Las Vegas ranch until the eleventh. This may suggest that Archie had discounted Henry's slanders. Perhaps Henry's attempt to browbeat Helen was the last straw that drove him into action.[14]

The grand jury had been seated on August 6, most of them men well known to the Stewarts who had done business with Archie and would continue these dealings with Helen. The trial began at ten o'clock in the morning August 11, with Henry, Kiel, and Helen the only witnesses. When questioned on the absence of other witnesses, Deputy Smith declared that Helen had not wanted any — a falsehood, as she had requested several. In the evening the jurors announced their verdict: all but one had voted to dismiss the charge. No transcript exists, but the length of the proceedings, despite the paucity of witnesses, suggests considerable disagreement. Six years later, in 1890, Parish would swing from the gallows in Ely for the murder of a miner he thought had laughed at him, and Helen would write in her Day Book on January 2, 1891: "First news of Hank Parishs Hanging," heavily underlining the last three words twice. Nonetheless, no one would ever be punished for Archibald Stewart's murder.[15]

Helen's Day Book entries during this difficult period principally record arrivals and departures at the ranch, of course a matter of some importance to the cook and hostess. Three catch the eye: the Indian, Mouse, employed by Helen and one day to be hated and feared as a dangerous renegade; James Wilson, a frequent visitor, sometimes with his half-Indian boys; and James Ross Megarrigle, a cultured man of many talents. Both Wilson and Megarrigle, in their different ways, would be especially meaningful to Helen in the time to come.

Sympathy for the young widow and her children seemed in short supply, both in El Dorado and Pioche. An account of the shooting in the *Mohave County Miner* implied that Archie had been shot by a former employee in a quarrel over wages. The men in El Dorado Canyon readily faulted Archie for the shooting, as his exacting business methods had made him many enemies. The article commented on the lack of sympathy for Stewart in the canyon, where most thought that he got what he had coming. In Pioche, the disposition to get even with Archie, now that he could not fight back, took even harsher form. On October 6, Helen applied to the Lincoln County Board of Equalization for the $1,000 tax exemption normally granted to widows. At the same meeting that granted the exemption, the county commissioners raised the assessment of the Stewart estate by $1,000, thereby negating the widow's tax exemption. Helen may have seethed within over this latest outrage, but she would not have been surprised. After the trial she had written her mother: "These county officials care but little wither justice is done so they reach the bottom of your pocket they are all right. **Money Money** is what all these fellows want."[16]

It was time to go home to Delia. When Helen returned to the farm in Galt in December 1884, very close to the time for the birth of her baby, she found the configuration of the family altered — perhaps more than appeared on the surface. Either the parental decree that the Wiser daughters must marry successful older men had been relaxed somewhat after Helen was safely married or Helen's younger sister Rachel had taken the bit in her teeth. In 1875, two years after Helen's marriage, she had married Andrew Shellard, age thirty-six, a carpenter in the mines of Gold Hill, Nevada. Helen's father, Hiram, clearly concerned about Helen, came to Las Vegas to look after the ranch during Helen's absence. He did a good deal to help her during the next few years while the children were still so young — Will, the oldest, was only ten at the time of Archie's death. Helen's Day Book often records trips by "Pa" and Will to El Dorado. She also writes about Hiram chasing after stock, planting alfalfa, and other ranch activities.[17]

Nonetheless, Delia remained at the center of the family, ever much concerned with the health, education, and advancement to "good positions" of her children and grandchildren. In her photo she appears to be in her forties, but she may have been older or younger. She seems ageless, the classic frontierswoman, her mouth wide and narrow, lips set firmly together with a downward turn that hints at disappointment, and dark far-seeing eyes.

Hers is a very determined face. No one and nothing, one feels, could stand in Delia's way. Safe in her mother's experienced hands, Helen gave birth on January 25, 1885, to a baby boy she named Archibald for his dead father. This fifth and last child was to be her favorite. When the baby had grown strong enough to travel, Helen and her children returned to the Las Vegas Ranch.[18]

The probate of the Stewart estate was completed in August, 1885. This comprised the ranch of 960 acres appraised at $8,000 and personal property consisting of horses, cattle, farming utensils, hay, and grain appraised at $2,000. This sum amounted to less than Archie had been offered for the ranch by the Californians. As soon as Helen completed a land grant begun by Archie, the ranch acreage expanded by half again as much to 1,460 acres, with surrounding range land as well. One half of the estate went to Helen, appointed guardian of her five children; the other half was divided equally among the children. Permission from the court on behalf of the children would be needed if Helen ever decided to sell. The court appointed Helen the administratrix of the estate and guardian of the children, with the authority to handle the children's interest in the estate with permission from the court. She nominated three competent and disinterested men to serve as appraisers, George Allen, James Wilson, and O. P. Bailey, duly appointed by the court and issued letters of administration. Simultaneously, Helen applied for her letter of administration of the estate. The appraisers estimated the personal property of the estate at $5,000 and did not anticipate that the value of the entire estate would exceed $20,000. As no one contested the application, the motion took effect as soon as Helen took the oath and filed a $10,000 bond. Joseph Eisenmann and D. C. Clark, both men who had done business with Archie and served as jurors when the grand jury convened, signed the bond with her. The three of them gave a surety of $5,000 in gold as a portion of the $10,000 bond. Creditors were given ten months to make claims on the estate before the settlement became final.[19]

More alone and more burdened than she had ever been, Helen resumed her place as mistress of the Mormon Trail.

# Chapter 4: *Coming Into Her Own*

Carrie B. Call was traveling from Salt Lake City to Los Angeles in a covered wagon with her husband, her infant son, her little niece, and a guide. On November 21, 1886, she unwrapped herself from the quilts bundled about her for warmth in the bitter cold and later wrote an entry in her diary: "we have bade the desert adieu I am happy to say. we are at Los Vegas ranch tonight. The lady here is very clever. She has given us a room with a fireplace in it ... It seems quite cheerful after the desert ... This is a lovely place. It is a large ranch. Mrs. Stewart the lady that owns this place has indians to work for her, both men and women. They raise apples, grapes, figs and almonds. We are having quite a gay time here. The lady and her children spent last evening with us and brought their refreshments with them, apples, pinyon nuts and raisins. The latter they raised and dried. we spent this eve with them and had some music on the guitar by yours truly. we brought the guitar along with us ... Mrs. Stewart's son has given me an arrow made by one of these indians."

"I wish we could take this comfortable little room along with us, but our guide thinks it would make our load too heavy." On leaving, Call wrote, "the people at the ranch seemed sorry to see us go. It is so seldom they see anyone."[1]

Carrie Call met Helen presiding in her customary role as gracious mistress of the trail. But she was not the same Helen as she had been when Archie was by her side. Of necessity she had been compelled to rise to the new role that her husband's murder had thrust upon her: proprietress of a large and valuable ranch; sole parent of five children ranging in age from the toddler, baby Archie, now almost two, to twelve-year-old Will, and all the financial decisions she must now make alone would affect their futures even more than her own. There were some she could turn to: Jim Wilson, a consistently close and ever dearer friend, and her father, Hiram, already hankering for a new life in southern Nevada. But essentially Helen was now alone in the remote desert that Archie had promised would be only their temporary home.

She rose to the occasion, finding abilities within herself that she had not known she possessed. There was a ranch to be run, so she ran it, although Archie had always been the rancher and she the housewife. There were important financial decisions to be made, so she made them, although secreting prospectors' monies behind the loose board had been all she had undertaken of finance. There was the pressing worry of the children's education in this remote valley far from any school, so presently she would solve that one, too.

Helen decided she would sell the ranch if possible, but only for a good price, for she was now the guardian of the children's patrimony. Archie would never have considered selling at a loss. Then, like the Gass family before her, she would move to a place in California where the children could attend school. To sell required permission from the court in Pioche. With her visiting parents serving as witnesses, Helen wrote a petition on October 29, 1885, to Judge Henry Rives requesting leave to sell because the isolated position of the ranch made it impossible for her family to remain there. She argued that she had no other place available for a home and no facilities to educate her children without "undue and unusual expense." The petition provides a glimpse of her assets in addition to the ranch itself: one gang plow, one reaper and mower, two old wagons, ten saddle horses, ten unbroken horses, one hundred and three cows, twenty-eight two-year-olds, forty yearlings, thirty tons of hay, four tons of barley, and fifteen hogs. Helen received her authorization to sell. What she did not have was a buyer.[2]

*Helen became the proprietress of a large enterprise and the sole parent of five children, as well as the mistress of the Mormon Trail.*
*Carrie Townley Porter*

Very well, until a well-heeled purchaser appeared, she would run the ranch herself. She would send to El Dorado bimonthly wagon shipments of two 500-600 pound butchered beeves, as well as hay, grains, vegetables, and fruit in season. On at least one occasion, Helen made the trip to El Dorado with her father to talk and bargain with a buyer herself. Sitting beside Hiram in the wagon, she saw slopes blanketed with cholla, single-stemmed cacti crowned with golden thorns as sharp as daggers, and hills topped with rocky outcroppings. They camped along the way. The smokestacks of the Southwestern Mining Company, mainstay of the district, came into view, along with the makeshift dwellings of a typical mining town not expected to last so long as it did. Approaching the blue Colorado River, rushing, surging, and racing down from the distant mountains, the road became so steep that a wagon driver had to use his hand brake or ride the wheel horse. Across the river rose the near Arizona mountains, sharply pointed, deeply scored with canyons, and black as though charred by infernal fires.

The Stewart wagon may not have been the only one on the road. Other suppliers, including the Kiels, also traded with El Dorado, and the Mormon farmers in the Moapa Valley sent their produce down the Colorado River to the camp by raft. El Dorado continued, as it had for more than twenty years, to be the stealth mining camp operating under the radar of the tax collector in Pioche. To avoid taxes, individual miners rarely reported their production, and the district's two large companies falsified their records to avoid taxes. Nonetheless, mining production is believed to have been substantial, and although population figures are similarly lacking, a considerable number of miners would have been necessary to perform the work; Helen estimated 150-200. This was fortunate because El Dorado provided her primary market.[3]

From October 1884 through May 1886, a principal figure in Helen's work force was the Southern Paiute, Mouse. Reportedly his name derived not from his stature, although he was small and slight, but from his manner, because he was "sly and keen" like a mouse. Communication with Mouse would have been easy for Helen because he spoke English fairly well, in addition to some Spanish; many Indians at the Las Vegas Ranch had a smattering of Spanish, which Helen ascribed to the influence of the Spanish padres who had passed through long before her time. In her Day Book, Helen frequently mentions work done by Mouse, bailing and hauling hay, pulling and hauling beans, hammering salt, and so forth, or payments made to him — more often than she makes note of other workers. This suggests unusual capabilities in Mouse and further suggests that, in keeping with her usual rapport with Indians, Helen had an amicable working relationship with him. She noted that Mouse had quit in May 1886, but apparently he continued to work for her in some capacity since she recorded paying Mouse "all due to date" in 1890. Because Indians were usually paid with supplies, this also indicates that Mouse was in a special category. His visit to show her his new horse nearly a year later suggests continued friendly relations. There is no evidence that Helen ever considered him a threat.[4]

The place of Mouse on the Stewart Ranch as a valued employee is particularly remarkable because in the spring of 1897 Mouse would become the object of a manhunt after he was accused of killing two prospectors in Arizona. While we do not hear Mouse's side, the story sounds damning indeed. After leaving Helen's employ, Mouse worked for a time for the ferryman Daniel Bonelli. According to George Perkins, a member of the posse that pursued him, he drank, "went berserk and wanted to kill someone." He became so feared and hated that even the Stewarts decided "it was best to try and get our own in." Hira, with a friend and several Indians, twice raided Mouse's camp without result. The other Indian workers fled for protection when Mouse started firing his six shooter. Bonelli discharged him and ferried him across the Colorado River to Arizona, where he worked as a freighter and odd job man in the White Hills Mining District. His wife, Mary, who might have exerted a restraining influence, had not accompanied him. Eventually, he "went berserk" again, stole a horse and rifle, traveled erratically back and forth across the river, and finally murdered two Arizona prospectors whom he had promised to lead to a rich gold ledge. In Perkins' words: "He was now a lone wolf, with a price on his head and hid out in the mountains alone. At times he would loot some lone prospector's camp for a little food and occasionally he would kill a mustang horse or a range steer, making the meat into jerky on which he lived."[5]

Because Mouse's violent deed was followed some three months later by the murders of five white miners in the vicinity of El Dorado by the Indian Ahvote and the purported flight to the mountains of several Indians, panic seized the region, undiminished by the circumstance that Ahvote was promptly killed. Nevada Governor Reinhold Sadler received telegrams from southern Nevada warning of a "general outbreak" by the Indians and requesting him to "arrange for troops" (Southern Nevada having no telegraph, these messages involved a time-consuming journey by buckboard to the nearest Arizona town with wire service); a Carson attorney offered to command the troops; Lincoln County Sheriff H. E. Freudenthal wrote also. Helen evidently knew the Indians too well to share the panic. She neither wrote the governor nor wired, apparently still believing that she and her family had nothing to fear from Mouse or any other Indian.[6]

Tracking Mouse through the country he knew so well in the vicinity of the Las Vegas Ranch long defeated the posse of Paiutes led by miner and prospector William Miller, who estimated that they traveled 500 difficult miles over five months. When Mouse did appear, ordinary citizens preferred not to confront him, although he had a reward on his head; on one occasion, he strolled through the streets of the town of Panaca unmolested. To lure him within reach of the posse, his son was brought to the Las Vegas Ranch. How Helen felt about using the youngster as bait on her ranch is unknown. When the Indian posse, described in the press as "impudent and saucy," paused at the ranch for two days, they may not have impressed her favorably.[7]

In late July the posse finally overtook and shot Mouse near Warm Springs. Perkins recalled that it was "almost impossible" to stop the Indians from repeatedly shooting at Mouse's dead body. After the inquest and the distribution of rewards, a rancher in the Moapa Valley asked them to throw the body in a shallow grave by the roadside "where he can yell at me when I pass that spot at night," which was done. Such was the world where Helen lived. To this day, the name of Helen's once valued employee turned renegade remains on the land at "Mouse's Tank," a pool of deep blue in the smooth bare, red sandstone in the

Valley of Fire where Mouse is believed to have paused in his flight.[8]

That a renegade Indian and a cultured Irish gentleman a bit down on his luck figured in Helen's life shows the wide diversity of her world during the years on the trail. Although the ranch prospered in her hands, the lack of education for the children deeply troubled Helen. She ingeniously engineered a solution by persuading James Ross Megarrigle, the teacher in the Moapa Valley, to move to the Las Vegas Ranch and tutor her children. Calling Megarrigle a teacher, however, was far from the sum of his accomplishments. Born in Ireland around 1827-28, he was said to have studied at Oxford (this may have been true or may merely have reflected the tendency among desert folk to mythologize the gifted). He followed the Gold Rush to California in 1850, intending to return and marry his fiancé when he had made his fortune. By 1860 he was mining in Quincy, California, not making his fortune, however. After ten years slipped past, his fiancé — known to us only as Mrs. M. Ford — followed him to America, but he did not join her in the Northeast, where she continued to await him.[9]

By 1870, Megarrigle ended up in southern Nevada, where he soon became indispensable. If the settlers needed oratory for a special occasion, the eloquent Megarrigle, well-endowed with the Irish gift of gab, was the man they turned to. If another shooting required a coroner to preside over the jury, as when the frontiersman Jack Longstreet shot Alexander Dry, Megarrigle filled the bill. As the closest thing to a lawyer in this remote world south of the third parallel, he performed many legal services, witnessing documents for Helen and others, writing a will for Conrad Kiel before the old man's death in 1894, and serving as a defense attorney in justice court. When a census of township, school district, or Civil War veterans came up, Megarrigle, now census taker (seven times over), was their man. He could also entertain a large audience by singing "choice selections from Pinafore"; the *Pioche Record* observed, "What a pity that such a voice as the Prof. has should be lost to the world amidst the sagebrush and sand hills of the Muddy." Despite his drinking and his hand-to-mouth existence, his charm and his many accomplishments made him popular with women. In the words of the *Pioche Record*, he "managed to elude a couple of his female admirers." He also eluded his fiancé. The patient Mrs. Ford waited twenty-four years before she despaired and married a close friend of Megarrigle's as the next best thing.[10]

Megarrigle moved to the Las Vegas Ranch and began tutoring the Stewart children in February 1889, no doubt to Helen's great relief. Now one intractable problem had been solved. Although the girls accepted instruction eagerly, the two older boys (now teenagers) resisted. Willie and Hira had attended school just briefly in Pioche before their move to the ranch, where Helen provided such education as they received. After doing men's work around the ranch for several years, they found it difficult to return to the roles of schoolboys. Helen urged them to attend and Delia strongly exhorted them: [Willie] "you are now or soon will be fifteen year you have missed all your primary classes I feel for you ... Now Willie you had ought to be now ready to take a position when you could comand $100 or more per month High what are you doing it is nice to idle your time when young but it kills you when you become a man so get right up and do something for your selve good you had ought to come with me by this time you would have been prety well Educated." Like many teenagers, the two boys disregarded sound advice. Because they much preferred working around the ranch to being tutored, their instruction lasted only a few days.[11]

Megarrigle, for his part, probably found a happy alternative to the uncertainties of his unsettled life at the Las Vegas Ranch in the hands of the kind and compassionate Helen. In addition to his invaluable services as a teacher, Megarrigle also was a delightful companion. She would one day write of him: "His goodness of heart and high intilectual qualites were held in great esteem by us his friends ... He was very kind and good and from the stores of knowledge held by a high order of intellect he was able to help his fellow beings and he never refused." He shared Helen's love of poetry, which they both wrote and she collected in a scrapbook. He played the violin, and aging though he might be, he still had the fine singing voice that the *Pioche Record* had opined should not be wasted on the sagebrush. Not least, he had the charm that so long inspired the devotion of Mrs. Ford.[12]

In 1893, Helen and Megarrigle organized a regular school, formally the first Las Vegas School District for Lincoln County. For a teacher to receive a salary from the state, a school needed a minimum of five pupils. To swell the ranks, Helen invited Jim Wilson's part-Indian boys to attend. In the 1893-1894 state report, Megarrigle received formal recognition as the first teacher in the Las Vegas School District and a salary of sixty dollars.[13]

Nonetheless, the school proceeded haltingly because Megarrigle's health was worsening — and not because he sometimes went "to wine," as Helen put it in her Day Book. In his late sixties and elderly by the standards of the nineteenth century, when most people died in their forties, he had contracted influenza, complicated by inflammatory rheumatism. Aware that he was dying, he gave Helen his only asset, his gold watch, to pay for his burial and asked her to notify Mrs. Ford. Although Helen nursed him tenderly, he died on March 16, 1894. Helen instead sent the watch to Mrs. Ford at her request, as a keepsake of the man she had awaited for twenty-four years and admitted loving in a way that "amounted to idolatry." It was a mark of Helen's warm friendship with James Ross Megarrigle that she buried him in the family plot known as the "Four Acres." Once again, she faced the matter of the children's education, especially the apple of her eye, little Archie, now nine-years-old.[14]

Megarrigle had been good company, not protection, but as the terror Helen had felt after her husband's murder sank to a subconscious level, her need for strong defenders also subsided. It is likely that she still had nightmares; she wrote of a particularly vivid one: "Dreamed someone told me George Anderson was killed with a bludgeon and robbed." All the same a fairly normal, if cool, relationship developed with Ed Kiel, who after all, had been absent in El Dorado on the day of Archie's death. In her Day Book, Helen heavily underlined Ed Kiel's name, usually a sign of her hatred, when he visited the Las Vegas Ranch in August, 1886, probably for the first time since the tragedy. Yet Ed Kiel stayed to dinner and evidently redeemed himself sufficiently that Helen no longer underlined his name when noting his comings and goings in September. On October 1, she wrote him a cool but civil note. "Mr. Ed Kiel Sir Please come and take your stock home as we intend gathering and branding. James Wilson is here after his stock and will take them home tomorrow," which she pointedly signed, "Mrs. Archie Stewart." In another note the following year, she primly reprimanded him, sounding more like a school marm than a frightened woman. "I send your mare home by Indian. Please keep her there. You will find it best to do what is right." Helen communicated only with Ed, never his father. Although she had reached an accommodation of sorts with the Kiels, her son Hira's animosity toward anyone named Kiel remained undiminished.[15]

Helen still expected a well-heeled purchaser for the ranch, and well-heeled he would need to be, in view of the price she had set. In May, 1887, A. C. Campbell, a Pioche businessman, considered buying it but withdrew. Two men from Haywood, California came in March, 1889, to inspect the ranch and discuss purchasing it. Helen's asking price had soared to $55,000, eleven times the sum for which Archie had acquired it in 1880, and included all stock and equipment. Unable to meet the price, they withdrew to Jim Wilson's Sand Stone Ranch after a four-day inspection.[16]

Meanwhile, the rhythms of ranch life continued. In September when the grapes ripened, they made wine, too great a temptation for some. Drunkenness in the work force was a recurrent problem for Helen. One such problem appearing in her Day Book in early 1887 was the notorious drinker John Bradfute, son of Colonel W. R. Bradfute, the official in charge of the Moapa Indian Reservation, also known for his heavy drinking. After Jack Longstreet, the mysterious desert frontiersman regarded as a leader by the Indians, denounced him to Washington authorities for his "totell disregard to the welfare of the indians," the elder

Bradfute was dismissed from his position. Because Helen no longer mentions the younger Bradfute or his frequent purchases of wine after March 1887, he may have drunk himself out of a job.[17]

Whether the men were drunk or sober, Helen had to see to it that ranch work proceeded on schedule. October was the month for picking apples, threshing wheat, baling hay, mending fences, breaking horses, and rounding up the stock. In January they pruned the grape vines, slaughtered hogs, and began the spring plowing. Vegetables were planted in February and fruit trees pruned. In April, they rounded up the stock and began branding the bawling calves. Traffic along the trail had grown lighter, and Helen duly noted slightly unusual travelers: "a man with a cross eyed girl," "a Dutchman and an Irishman," "two donkeys and three Englishmen," "Jipsy woman here and boy." Helen made one attempt through the good offices of Jim Wilson to trade with Ivanpah, a silver camp forty-nine miles southwest of Las Vegas. Knowing the country well, Wilson would not have found it so arduous a trip as did

Carrie Call, who wrote in her diary that her family had been advised "no matter which way we went we would wish we had gone the other." Helen judged the returns that Wilson brought back not worth the trip. Ivanpah had gone into a downward tailspin, and El Dorado remained her mainstay.[18]

Etched on the glass wall of the orientation room of the Old Las Vegas Mormon Fort State Historic Park is a famous quote from Helen. She often told her children just to be patient, for civilization would find them, that she could see the glint of the rails, the smoke of the trains, and the homes and church spires in the grain field on the hill.

CHAPTER 4: COMING INTO HER OWN

For some time, she and her father had been pursuing a long-standing American tradition since colonial times — land speculation. As historian Richard White points out, far from being invariably opposed, the rancher and the land speculator were often the "same person." At the same time, as Silver Mountain had shown, Hiram remained susceptible to prospecting. After an absence of several months, he set off on a prospecting expedition with three other men in late September, 1886, returning empty-handed a month later. So far, Helen was immune to his passion for mining. Some women prospectors, obsessed as Hiram, were already scouring the desert hills in search of bonanza, but despite the discovery of silver Spanish coins dated 1770 on the Las Vegas Ranch, Helen did not fantasize about Spanish gold. Though she eventually invested in several mines, this remained merely a facet of her evolution into a business-woman taking advantage of the available opportunities.[19]

Rumors about building a railroad through the Moapa Valley, the Las Vegas Valley, and other areas in Lincoln County gained new credence with the arrival of a team of surveyors in September 1889 working through these areas and as far west as the California-Nevada border. This triggered a surge of land acquisitions, as Helen's invest-ments accelerated and out-of-state promoters seized the chance for profit. During the eight month period ending in May, over 25,000 acres were claimed in the southern portion of the county, mostly by outside interests. One San Franciscan entered 13,000 acres under the Desert Land Act; the original legislation, passed by Congress in 1876 in an attempt to foster irrigation in the arid West, lent itself to fraud because speculators could plow a few furrows and assert that the legal requirement for irrigation had been met.[20]

Despite the petty transactions carefully recorded in her Day Book, Helen had accumulated enough cash for land purchases, and her family rallied around to help her. Commonly, as with mining claims, when someone wanted more than the provisions of law allowed, a claim under another's name would be filed and later transferred to the party who sought the land. In 1897, Helen's sister Asenath, married to an Irishman, James Roach, helped Helen with one of these maneuvers, using funds from Helen to file two applications for land, quickly transferred to Helen, who had funded the original purchase.[21]

From 1888 through the nineties Helen and Hiram Wiser bought large tracts of land. Wiser acquired part of the land, long afterward known as the Wiser Ranch, from Jack Longstreet. As he prepared to head farther west into wilder, less populated country in Oasis Valley (near present Beatty), Longstreet had allowed his Moapa Valley ranch to slide onto the delinquent tax list. Owing the county more than $600, he sold Wiser the 240-acre spread of the best land in the valley for $1,200 in September 1888. Probably the reasons for this purchase were several. Hiram was always ready for a new challenge; this place offered a handy base for prospecting; and most of all, he may have wanted to be nearby when Helen needed him. Wiser then bought additional land in the names of various family members. Believing that Helen wanted to sell the Las Vegas Ranch, Delia also was eager to participate. In July 1887, she wrote asking her daughter to "give me a chance " to rustle up a buyer for $15,000 and make some money. Helen, of course, had set her sights much higher.[22] Although both parents visited Helen in the autumn of 1885, Delia would not be joining Hiram in the Moapa.

At the same time, Helen undertook an innovation, with family help, that changed the management of the Las Vegas Ranch stock from the simple pattern of raising and selling to El Dorado that prevailed in her husband's time and also continued her efforts to diversify the marketing. She made an arrangement with her father and her brother-in-law, Ed , newly married to her sister Flora. They would undertake a two-year lease for one hundred head of her cows, from two-year-olds to the oldest, and drive them to Wiser's ranch on the Muddy River. Wiser and Ed would receive half the increase when the cows calved and pay all taxes on the cattle. This deal was renewed as needed until Helen executed a new lease in 1894 with her father and another brother-in-law, Andrew Shellard (Rachel's husband). This time Wiser and Shellard would take 166 head of Helen's cattle, including eighty cows expected to calve that year, and would keep one-third of the increase over the next two years; Helen would pay the taxes, provide hands to help with branding, and take back cattle for her beef sales, excepting those with calves. This arrangement benefitted both parties. Wiser started his herd with very little expense, and they thrived so well that when he drove 275 head to Utah in the spring of 1897, they were acknowledged to be good-sized animals, unlike many raised in the hot desert climate. Helen benefitted because she now needed fewer hands to care for the cattle, by no means an unimportant consideration.[23]

Absorbing as land deals, ranch management, and family cares might be, there was still an emptiness in Helen. Archie was probably the love of her life, but he was long dead, and she was a young woman, only in her mid-thirties and still in her prime. She needed to be loved by a man again, and attentive Jim Wilson was always there for her. Frequently visiting the ranch, at times with his boys, Tweed and Jim Jr., often alone, never absent for more than a short time, he probably had loved her for years. Although a family recollection on the relationship is explicit, other evidence is slight, and the beginning and the end of the affair cannot readily be pinpointed.[24]

*Jim Wilson and his sons, Tweed and James at the Sand Stone Ranch. (Spring Mountain State Park)*
*Photo, Spring Mountain Ranch*

Perhaps the February 19, 1889, notation in Helen's Day

Book, "Jim Wilson came down 'Oh, do take care'" signified a warning to herself at the beginning. Finding enough privacy for a tryst would have been difficult, with the ranch house small and always busy. The ranch was large, however, and offered places where a couple might ride out to be alone together. Perhaps the peach orchard in spring, with pink blossoms sifting down. Perhaps among the sweet-smelling willows. From Helen's Day Book, we know the relationship was more than platonic because Helen, fearing pregnancy, wrote tiny letters in her book on January 14, 1891, indicating her "egg passed. Safe." High on a rocky crag in Sand Stone Ranch someone carved the name "Helen." Could it have been a man in his fifties, already rheumatic, smitten as the lovesick teenagers who cut the names of their girlfriends on trees inside a heart shape or spray them as graffiti on walls?[25]

Would they marry? Jim Wilson undoubtedly hoped so. The last clue surfaces in a letter. Wilson remained in touch with his family, rafts of nieces and nephews, as well as siblings, and had gone back to Ohio to visit them in 1881. To these relatives, he was an exotic figure leading a dangerous life in the "wilds of Nevada." "I feared you was among the slain," wrote one of his sisters, having read about the hostile Indians committing "so many bloody massacrees"; "I did not know but that you had starved to death way off our therre as there has been some talk bout the western folks not having very much to eat or drink," a niece wrote, "But I could bet on your drink all the same, Eh!" Buried amidst the concerns over Wilson's safety, the family news, and the requests for money that constitute the bulk of the correspondence, appears a letter indicating that Wilson had mentioned Helen to his family and hinted at his hopes.

His niece Jennie Clark wrote on March 8, 1891: "we have not herd from you for a great while and maby you have got married. The last letter you wrote you said you was invited to a nice little widows to a party and she had a great deal of money maby you got her."[26]

But to Helen's son, sixteen-year-old Hira, who had somehow learned of the affair despite his mother's discretion, getting the nice (and rich) little widow was no teasing matter. He did not want his mother to remarry — ever — and because of the half-Indian children, Wilson may have been especially distasteful to him. The general understanding has been that Wilson's partner, George Anderson, had fathered the children, but some may have whispered that it was Wilson, and Hiram could have shared this opinion. Although earlier reported dead, Annie is listed as Wilson's wife in the 1880 census, and her youngest son, James, is only nine-months-old. Anderson having left for California in 1879, fatherhood by either man seems possible. Annie and a little daughter either subsequently died or left the area, leaving the two boys, John Twison (known as Tweed) and little Jim Jr., both of whom Wilson reared as his own and gave his name to. Helen, knowing her second son's black moods, took his opposition seriously, and eventually drifted apart from her lover. Perhaps she was remembering Jim when she wrote her daughter Tiza many years later near the end of her life:

"I have been in love with a man and know how blindly one follows the flickering FLAME untill it gradually fades out or dies out from neglect or as the old saying 'Time Silence and Absence are pitiless destructives. Well love is a delightful experience They say it is Better To Have Loved and Lost than never to have loved atall. I think it is a delightful delirium from which it is a pity to be awakened at any time. So if you are in love feed the Flame and love on."[27]

HELEN J. STEWART: FIRST LADY OF LAS VEGAS

# Chapter 5: *Helen's World*

Although the scattered population of southern Nevada remained too sparse to support a newspaper, Helen would have heard about the affray at the Chispa Mine in the summer of 1895 by word of mouth. Rumors could spread more quickly than news reports and exceed the printed word in sensational excess. The scene was a new boom on the western side of the Spring Mountains in the Montgomery Mining District that contained the Chispa and Johnnie mines. While a Mormon mining company in Utah had just bought a large interest in both, the leading figures were still the brothers George and Bob Montgomery, a situation disputed by the former mine superintendent, Angus McArthur. He contended that the Montgomerys' claim had lapsed during a period of inactivity, and he attempted a claim jumping at the Chispa with several hired guns.[1]

Helen would have listened to the story with interest because she had some acquaintance with at least three of those involved, as was inevitable in the small closed world of southern Nevada. She certainly knew the claim jumper in chief, Angus McArthur, as a gracious host. On the preceding Fourth of July, the Stewart family had joined the entire population of the Las Vegas Valley — and some from far beyond — for a three-day celebration at the Yount Ranch, home of the Harsha Whites. The settlers danced until after midnight, when the Fourth was ushered in with shooting pistols and an anvil salute. The afternoon of the big day passed with foot races, sack races, rock races, egg races, national songs, and an exhibition of turning and jumping on the bar by John Yount. After more dancing, a feast for fifty people was served. The next day

McArthur invited the assemblage to his Pahrump ranch six miles away to spend the evening and enjoy a meal at one o'clock in the morning. Helen also knew another member of what the press termed McArthur's "private army" — Jack Longstreet, when she served as his "attorney-in-fact" to clarify the title to her father's Moapa ranch. Difficult as it is to imagine the last desert frontiersman, with his long hair, his severed ear, and his notched Colt. 44, sitting down with the refined Helen to discuss the matter, they may have been quite congenial. Meeting a real lady brought out Longstreet's southern courtliness, and Helen might have been impressed by his charismatic presence and tales she had heard of his adventures. Nonetheless, the claim jumper who must have most surprised her was Phil Foote. He had so affected Helen that she later wrote an essay about meeting him (undated but typewritten).[2]

On a spring day Helen was sitting on her porch facing the trail shelling peas when "a dapper appearing man of a soldierly appearance, rode up to the weeping willow near the road and dismounting from one of two beautiful sorrel horses" approached her. "The man attracted me particularly; as being a type of man who had dared much and suffered much and lost much; but yet dareing eneough to try the fiat of fate; He was the blonde Type with a clear grey eye, face clear clean and ruddy, hair slightly inclined to wave over a good broad forehead; He interested me at once, he looked like a soldier brave who had fought and won many a battle." (Actually, he was a gambler who had lost and won many a pot.)

Foote sat beside Helen and helped her shell peas, while telling her his story, much painted up for the edification of a lady listening with rapt attention. He related that he had left his peaceful eastern home when a "spirit of adventure seemed to take possession of me and drive me to the West." He landed in Leadville, where "everything was excitement, and Gambling, and drinking, and all the excesses of life were rife." He soon became marshal of the nearby mining town of "Co-co-mo," handily subduing toughs, then drifted from one mining town to another in search of treasure.

After a lucky strike near Park City, he briefly returned to his family in the East, where he married a beautiful Christian woman of "High Purpose." When mining fever struck again, she accompanied him back to Utah. Unsuccessful in his mining efforts, he tried gambling. Following a losing streak at faro, he "became consumed with the desire for money no matter how" and robbed a faro table bank in one of the gambling houses. Turning over the stolen money to his wife, he left and his daring escape from a posse ensued. Helen swallowed his story whole.[3]

Apparently lunch intervened before Foote could relate his version of the denouement nor tell what became of the beautiful Christian woman of "High Purpose." According to a newspaper report, he turned himself in and served a year in jail. The claim jumping at the Chispa would not be another episode to be related to an admiring lady while shelling peas on her porch. McArthur's hired guns, Foote, Longstreet, and George Morris, seized the Chispa Mine easily enough and holed themselves up there. The press anticipated a "long siege." But the Montgomerys had other plans. They ordered two cases of rifles from Los Angeles and hired a Texas sharpshooter. Then they attacked with a well-armed force of miners, taking the claim jumpers completely by surprise while they were having breakfast.

The only casualty was Phil Foote, shot in the chest. Perhaps recognizing an untenable situation and hoping to relieve Foote's suffering with medical help or morphine, the claim jumpers surrendered. Foote nonetheless died. The newspaper commented upon him less romantically than Helen. "He lived for the reputation of a dead game man and he played the string out."[4]

When the law arrived, Longstreet and Morris submitted to arrest on the trumped up charge of "drawing and exhibiting" deadly weapons and in court they were fined exorbitant sums. This must have amused many, because well they knew that most men in the region carried guns. Even if Helen soon heard that the handsome man who charmed her was best described as an ex-con and claim jumper, she must have retained her high regard for him — or she would not have written his version of his life.[5]

Romance and tragedy altered Helen's world over the next few years. Although the still sparse population of the area included few eligible young women, both Will and Hira found brides. Will's was German-born Lena Carl. After her family converted to Mormonism, they emigrated to Utah, where Lena's mother remarried, later moving on to the Moapa Valley. It seems doubtful that Lena was a practicing Mormon, or she would not have encouraged the attentions of a boy outside the church. She met him when he visited a ranch on the Muddy River belonging to his grandfather — Hiram Wiser. Will Stewart and Lena became better acquainted in 1891 when Lena accompanied her family on a visit to the Stewart Ranch. She stayed on to help the Stewart children with the cooking while Helen recovered from "la grippe."[6]

It seems likely that the pair had been sweethearts for

HELEN J. STEWART: FIRST LADY OF LAS VEGAS

some time before they married on October 5, 1891, in the Moapa Valley when he was twenty-one and she was nineteen. To modern eyes dazzled by wedding planners and lavish events, it may seem odd that no family member apparently accompanied them. The simple wedding, however, was a common pioneer custom, not necessarily a signal of estrangement. The bridal couple then moved in with Helen at the ranch. A letter to Helen several years later from Lena, written in a good, clear hand with none of the mistakes in spelling and grammar so prevalent in the period, suggests that Lena was a young woman of some education. Although Lena signs the letter, "Lovingly," she apparently never developed a close relationship with Helen.[7]

James Megarrigle's death left a vacancy for a teacher in the Las Vegas School District. In 1895 Dreeme Gann, the only Lincoln County applicant to pass the state examination for teachers, took the position to instruct eight pupils. Dreeme's name suggests a family penchant for fanciful naming; she had an older sister Demonia, and her mother (though known as Birdie) had been named Prairie Bird, not an unsuitable appellation, because like Helen herself, as well as Jim Wilson and the Kiels, the Ganns had roots in the Midwest. Birdie liked to tell that Abraham Lincoln had split logs for her grandfather. The Gann family moved from El Dorado to St. Joseph in the Moapa Valley. There they acquired considerable land, gradually selling it to incoming settlers. They also farmed, raising hay and other products, as well as ranging cattle.[8]

When Dreeme took up her teaching duties at the ranch, Hira was serving as clerk of the school district. Proximity led to courtship, and this time signs appeared of family involvement, perhaps because the Stewart and Gann families were becoming very close; indeed Helen and Birdie remained dear friends for life. At the ceremony on December 5, 1896, when Dreeme was twenty-two and Hira twenty-one, William Harris, Justice of the Peace for the St. Joseph District, officiated at the ranch, with Tiza as one of the witnesses. Again, the young couple moved in at the ranch. Helen made little comment on the new arrangements in her expanded household.[9]

The establishment of the Las Vegas School District reflected the rise of the ranch as the hub of the region. In 1890 the Stewart Ranch became the Las Vegas voting precinct — again. Earlier attempts had failed when only three voters appeared in 1874. Voters then were obliged to cast their ballots in El Dorado until 1888 when Jim Wilson's ranch briefly served as the Sand Stone precinct, superceded by the Las Vegas Ranch two years later.[10]

Helen's appointment as postmaster in 1893 further enhanced the importance of the Las Vegas Ranch. Prior to this, mail had traveled from Pioche by a circuitous route, stopping at St. Thomas, then down to El Dorado and back to Las Vegas. When the auditor for the U.S. Treasury inquired in 1894 why Las Vegas had not submitted a report, Helen responded that she had nothing to report. Being fifty miles by wagon road from the nearest post office, she had not yet been able to fill the contract for mail delivery. Her difficulties underscored the remoteness of the region.[11]

Helen once hinted at regret that Will and Hira were not "settled in business yet." In fact, she was fortunate that the older boys made running the ranch their business at a time when land purchases, cattle sales, and the education of the younger children in southern California preoccupied her.

Will shouldered the farming side of the ranch enterprise. He had begun this work when very young, accompanying his father on trips to El Dorado when he was only ten. After his father's death, he continued the canyon trips with a hired hand or his grandfather. Will baled hay, pruned trees, irrigated, maintained the plows and other machinery, and repaired the ranch buildings. He spent his seventeenth birthday burning grass in the fields.[12]

At the same time, Hira concentrated on the ranching side of the operation. At fourteen he was rounding up beeves for slaughter and also participating in the slaughter. By 1898, he was much involved in cattle sales. He held out for a higher price from visiting Wyoming cattle buyers, which suggested that he may have inherited some of his late father's business acumen. When the buyers offered $12 for yearlings, Hira wanted $13. He raised the price from $15 for two-year-olds to $17, and from $16 for dry cows to $20. After the completion of this large sale in February 1898 with Helen's concurrence, Hira accompanied the buyers to the Muddy where the cattle were ranging and helped them select their herd. He then escorted them as far as Cane Springs.[13]

Relying on the boys, Helen devoted herself to the effort to educate the younger children, her adored little Archie (then twelve) and Eva (then fifteen), both under the wing of Tiza (then eighteen). In 1897 Helen arranged for them to board, attend school, and receive evening tutoring in Los Angeles, where Eva would also study music. The girls did carry on with their studies as Helen intended, but so far as can be determined, Archie did not attend the Norwood School as planned. When Helen was obliged to return to the ranch, she missed them acutely and worried about them incessantly.[14]

*Archie, Jr. (1897), Helen's youngest child
and her favorite.
Nevada State Museum Las Vegas*

These worries frequently recur in her letters after she returned to the ranch for a big cattle sale. She exhorted Archie: "My boy if you love me try and learn;" "Dont go with rough boys;" "Be neat and clean and orderly;" "Be good and careful. Dont waste time nor be careless of yourselves;" "Since I came home I have been looking with disgust on these ignorant poor fellows who haven't a cent to their names and don't know enough to take care of themselves. Let alone taking care of any one else;" "I will need your help badly. So you must learn so you will know how to help;" And above all, "Be careful to turn off the Gass in your rooms. Never forget and blow it out. You see that would leave the gass jet open and fill the room with Gas, which if the windows were closed would be sure to cause you death."[15]

Helen's worries must have intensified when she learned of Archie's Thanksgiving adventure, recounted in two southern California newspapers. Archie had slipped out of the house on Thanksgiving morning without telling anyone. Encountering a friend, Pete Cochran, Archie accompanied him to Pasadena, where they became separated. When it grew late, Archie went to the police station, where he told his story. At first, the marshal thought he had escaped from the reform school and tried to get him to admit it. During questioning, the marshal learned that the boy had eaten nothing all day, so he took him to his own home, where he joined the marshal's family for Thanksgiving dinner.

After dinner the marshal telephoned the Los Angeles chief of police, who sent an officer to the home where the children boarded, a great relief for Tiza and Eva, and their friends. They had been searching for Archie since morning. They hurriedly retrieved their adventurous and imaginative little brother. One of the newspaper reporters present in the marshal's office related that Archie had set out on foot to rejoin his mother, a large property owner in Nevada. When a reporter interviewed the sisters, they denied this, explaining that "Archie was very anxious to go east with mother, and was rather spunky when he was not permitted to do so. That is all there is to it." Obviously exasperated, they added that their brother was "a prodigious liar." In her letter to Helen, Tiza explained that the presence of a newspaper reporter had encouraged Archie to embellish his story, and his experience had taught him "a lesson he will not soon forget."[16]

Not only did Archie know how to spin a fine tale, but also he knew the way to a woman's heart, and not with the usual feminine fripperies. Before Tiza left the ranch to join him in Los Angeles, he had sent her a gift that he thought would give her many hours of pleasure — 800 cartridges. He knew that young women at the ranch much enjoyed walking beside the Las Vegas Creek and shooting ducks. Tiza well deserved those cartridges. Helen wrote to her oldest daughter: "I apreciate you much more than you realize Tiza I know you are a little bundle of the truest womanly material that was ever put together. Others appreciate the same fact and know it."[17]

Helen could count herself fortunate, not only for the help of the older boys at the ranch, but also for care of the younger children in Los Angeles. Their devotion to Helen and their willingness to pitch in when needed showed the close ties that had developed between them during her many years as a single parent. Helen appears to have been land rich and cash poor at this time. Although she longed to join the younger children in Los Angeles, important cattle sales that would bring her the cash to continue their education obliged her to remain at the ranch. She even considered selling at a loss "to be sure of enough money for you to have what you need," an idea she presently rejected. At last, with Hira's help, she closed the deal with the Wyoming cattle buyers and could joyfully write, "Hurrah for Los Angeles and the children I love!"[18]

The year 1898 brought two life-changing events. First, the death in May of Helen's father, Hiram Wiser, in Downey,

HELEN J. STEWART: FIRST LADY OF LAS VEGAS

California, near Los Angeles. What brought Hiram to Downey and what malady or accident had ended the life of this tough old pioneer at seventy-one remain unknown. So, too, do Helen's feelings about the loss of the father, who had moved near her after Archie's death and helped her in many ways, leaving her mother and the pleasant life of Galt behind. Helen's Day Book provides no answers because it ends in 1892. Either she ceased keeping Day Books or those she kept have not been preserved. Unless letters or recollections provide a clue, some questions remain unanswered. The other notable event in that year was the arrival of Helen's first grandchild, Leslie, born to Hira and Dreeme in October and a delight to his grand-mother. "Little Leslie is as cute as he can be," she wrote to Tiza when the baby was eight-months-old. "He knows as much as some grown people."[19]

Even a cute grandchild did not dent Helen's adoration of little Archie. On the occasion of his birthday, January 25, 1899, she wrote him: "This is your birthday. You are fourteen-years-old. I wonder what course you will pursue. What will you do? What kind of man you will be. I think you have pride and manliness about you to try and be one of the best. Remember always I love you and always think of you every day and wonder what you are doing.

Dare to do right,
Dare to be true,
Dare to do good,
Everything will come right for you."[20]

Archie had no chance to answer these questions. His fourteenth birthday was his last one. While chasing wild horses at the ranch in July, he suffered a fatal fall from his horse. Helen was grief-stricken. She buried the child, her pride and joy, just north of the father he had never seen. She could not be comforted. On January 25, 1900, the day that would have been Archie's fifteenth birthday, she wrote a tear-stained letter to Tiza. "Today Archie would have been fifteen years old. I have cried most all day through my work and all. I have had a dreadful time bringing myself to submit to what I know must be. I needed him so much." Years would pass before she could write a friend in a 1907 condolence letter, "I had other children to live for." Perhaps her sorrow made this normally strong and self-reliant woman especially vulnerable.[21]

The year 1900 saw a violent end to one of the earliest pioneer families in the Las Vegas Valley, an end that legend connected with the Stewarts. After Conrad Kiel's death in 1894, his son Ed had inherited the ranch. In 1900 William, Ed's younger brother, arrived from the Midwest to live with him. This arrangement proved disastrous, and ill feelings between the brothers became widely known. On October 11, Will Stewart and Frank Stewart (an employee and no relation) went to the Kiel Ranch to buy tobacco and inform Ed that some wagon wheels had arrived at the Manvel railroad station. As they approached the small grove of poplars, the familiar one-story board "blue house," the slightly larger "brown house," also of board, and the old adobe came into view. Then they saw something unfamiliar — the front and back doors of the ranch house stood open. They saw Ed Kiel prostrate on the kitchen floor, a pistol near his right hand. They then found William Kiel lying about thirty feet away across a ditch, his body partly submerged in the water and a double-barreled shotgun near his feet. Touching nothing, they returned to the Stewart Ranch to report the crime. A guard kept watch over the bodies until a coroner's jury could be assembled on October 13.[22]

*The three room adobe ranch house where the Stewarts lived in 1882 gained some additions by 1902, including the bedrooms at left. The building behind the ranch house is still extant.*
*Nevada State Museum Las Vegas*

Helen — perhaps significantly — had been away on a trip to San Francisco at the time of the killings. She arrived home the night before the bodies were found. She wrote letters summoning C.M. Over, Justice of the Peace of the Goodsprings District, to preside at the inquest and Jim Wilson, still someone she automatically turned to in emergencies, despite his advancing age and ill health. During the inquest, members of the jury, including Wilson, listened to testimony. Ed Kiel's only injury was a gunshot wound above the right eye. Several injuries had been inflicted upon William Kiel: a gunshot wound in the left arm between the elbow and wrist had broken his arm bones; a second gunshot wound passed entirely through the center of his body; a third, near the left eye, had passed through his brain. Four shots had recently been fired from the pistol lying near Ed, leaving two cartridges. Three shots were surmised to have been the bullets that struck William and the fourth the one that killed Ed, leaving powder burns on his hat and face and slicing his hat. The pistol lay where it would naturally have fallen if Ed had shot himself. The shotgun near William's feet contained no shells, nor had it recently been fired.[23]

Frank and Will Stewart were the only witnesses called by the jury. Frank related that only a few days before the killing Ed had told him that he planned to run William off the ranch. He felt William was "no good" and had no interest in the ranch. On the other hand, William had confided to Frank that he did not get along with Ed, felt no affection for his brother, and planned to leave the ranch. Questioned about the Kiels' drinking habits, Frank testified that Ed drank heavily, while William was not far behind. Will Stewart confirmed Frank's testimony.[24]

The jury concluded that the deaths were an open-and-shut case of murder and suicide by Ed Kiel, yet stories implicating Hira persisted, strengthened by his known black streak. The emotions he had felt as a boy standing beside his murdered father's grave had not faded over the years. Instead, his grief and anger had deepened into obsession. One legend tells that he had finally decided to take revenge on the Kiels. To avoid suspicious tracks, he tied horseshoes to his feet and walked to the Kiel ranch house, so people said.

Those concurring with the jury's verdict could raise several objections to this legend. Neither Kiel could have played a part in Archie Stewart's death: Ed was then absent in El Dorado and William still lived in the Midwest. Their only possible crime was bearing the Kiel name, and that seems far-fetched. It is difficult to imagine that Hira would wait so long for retribution, and equally hard to imagine that Hira could have caught the Kiels unawares and murdered them. The bullet that killed Ed would have required the shooter to stand right next to him and place the gun close to his head. What experienced man having Ed's reputation and long experience in dealing with gunslingers and desperados could have been duped into a situation where someone could kill him at close range?

Support for the legend of the murder of both Kiels comes from an unexpected source — modern science. In 1975 it became necessary to exhume the graves in the private cemetery on the Kiel Ranch to allow the sale of the site. As circumstances required, the exhumation under the direction of archeologist Dr. Richard Brooks and physical anthropologist Dr. Sheilagh Brooks was accomplished in a single day, but with the permission of the Kiel family, the skeletal remains were examined and x-rayed in the physical anthropology laboratory, where additional experts, Dr. Raymond Rawson, a dentist, and Dr. Sheldon Green, assistant Clark County Coroner, also studied them. In addition, the Brookses took the Kiel brothers' skulls to the 1976 American Academy of Forensic Sciences meetings, where colleagues confirmed their findings. The verdict, subsequently published in a study on forensic anthropology, was unanimous, "murder by a person or persons unknown." The direction of the shots figured centrally in this conclusion. Edward Kiel was probably ambushed as he walked out of the ranch house and shot from the rear by a .44 or .45 revolver, and William was shot twice, from different angles, with a shotgun as he came toward the murderer. In Sheilagh Brooks words: "We believe that Edward was shot first by someone he knew and then William came running. He was shot as he was coming across the creek with shotguns. Apparently a .45-caliber pistol and a shotgun or shotguns were used in both murders." Science could not, of course, identify the killer.[25]

The last word came from Henry Lee, a rancher from Panaca and an aspiring politician. As a young man he had spent a good deal of time at the Stewart Ranch and knew the family well. He stated unequivocally two years before his death in 1973: "I figured Hi did it, Hi Stewart. I don't think there's a doubt in the world of it. He was the most reckless one of the family."[26]

The Kiels had made little effort to develop the ranch, as the inventory of the estate confirmed. Ed left one horse, ten head of cattle, a few farm implements and store goods, fifty acres of improved land, and 190 acres of unimproved desert land. William left one nickel watch and chain and

HELEN J. STEWART: FIRST LADY OF LAS VEGAS

a tobacco sack containing twenty-one dollars in coin. "Ed Kiel's siblings who lived in the Midwest inherited the estate. Hampton George, husband of Conrad Kiel's grandaughter, Sadie, served as administrator."

The couple lived in Los Angeles and had been warm friends of Helen's for several years. Under subsequent owners, the rundown Kiel Ranch became a showplace, with a gracious white home and a sweeping tree-lined drive superseding the derelict old buildings and the handful of poplars. Finally, it morphed into the Boulderado Dude Ranch, where Hollywood celebrities and other guests enjoyed swim parties at the pool and moonlight horseback rides.[27]

Frank Stewart began appearing in Helen's correspondence in 1897. Although some have stated that he was the foreman at the Las Vegas Ranch, this was not the case. Born in Pennsylvania on December 28, 1850, Frank Royer Stewart had led the life of a rolling stone, keeping stores or mining at various small towns, mostly in southern California, never staying long in one place. Finally by 1890, he came to rest at the Las Vegas Ranch, where he kept the books and tended the post office. In fact, the position of foreman probably did not exist at the ranch. Helen closely managed the ranch herself, aided by Will and Hira as they matured.

Nonetheless, Frank was no ordinary employee. When Helen listed "the folks on the ranch now," (1898) Frank was one of only two who were not family members. When little Archie was in Los Angeles, he wanted Frank to write, and Helen urged the youngster to go every Saturday to spend time with Frank's brother Madison, a merchant who "stands very high in the minds of his fellow men." This raises the possibility that, in addition to improving Archie, some of the luster of the esteemed Madison might elevate the status of Frank. As Archie lay ill at the ranch the month before his fatal fall, much worrying his mother, she wrote Tiza. "Mr. Stewart was very kind to help me while Archie was sick and has been very kind since. He has helped me put up six gallons of Plum Preserves and about five gallons of Apple Jelly. Besides a lot of dried apples."[28]

He became important to her for more than assistance in canning, and the following year he apparently began playing hard to get. A friend reassured her: "I am sorry to hear that my friend Mr. F Stewart contemplates leaving the Vegas. He is a good man. I am sorry for your sake also. But I am of the opinion that he will not go. So do not worry over it." If Frank was insisting upon marriage, subsequent events indicated that a large obstacle stood in the way.[29]

HELEN J. STEWART: FIRST LADY OF LAS VEGAS

# Chapter 6: *The End of an Era*

In 1901, the event Helen had long been preparing for arrived. Railroad surveyors had appeared in the Las Vegas Valley in 1889, and Helen had joined the land rush, using her available funds to buy more properties. A dozen years later the great expectations of these investors seemed on the verge of realization when building a line south from Salt Lake City to southern California along the old Mormon Trail became an active interest for not one but two railroad titans, Edward Harriman and William Clark.

They had strong reasons to be interested. Harriman was first, last, and foremost a railroad man. He had made the Union Pacific into a paragon of a railroad and gained control of the mighty Southern Pacific. Added to his subsidiary railroads, including the Oregon Short Line, he aimed at nothing less than control of the railroads in the entire central western and southwestern U.S. William Clark, the Montana copper king who opposed him, harbored no less sweeping ambitions for his proposed San Pedro, Los Angeles, and Salt Lake Railroad. Not only would he control the southbound traffic, gain access to southern Utah mining developments, and shorten the distance for his copper shipments by 663 miles, but also the concept appealed to his pride. He had finally gained the seat in the U.S. Senate that he had coveted during several disgraceful campaigns involving blatant bribery and even the invalidation of his appointment. It has been suggested that he wanted to be remembered as someone other than the multimillionaire who tried to buy his way into the Senate. Rather, he would like to be known as the builder of a great empire in the American West.[1]

*William Clark speaking from a railroad car.*
*UNLV Special Collections*

The absence of a route south from Salt Lake City created a blank space in the network of western railroads that made it especially appealing to empire builders. Northern Nevada had been well served by railroads that also rigidly controlled state politics. The mighty Central Pacific (later Southern Pacific), joining the east and west, had crossed Nevada since 1869. Lesser railroads, such as the Virginia and Truckee and the Carson and Colorado, dangled southward. Soon the Tonopah and Goldfield would be constructed to tie the Southern Pacific to the central Nevada mining booms at Tonopah and Goldfield. In 1901, however, the boom was still in its infancy. Tonopah had just been discovered in 1900, and Goldfield, destined to be the

HELEN J. STEWART: FIRST LADY OF LAS VEGAS

greatest frenzy of all, was only a gleam in a prospector's eye. Still, it seems not unlikely that a touch of the Tonopah excitement quickened the pulses of railroad men in 1901.[2]

Harriman was the first to bite. Helen was ready. Her sons had already deeded their portions of the estate to her for one dollar each plus "love and affection" in order to simplify the sale; of course, she would give them their portions as planned after the sale went through. In the spring of 1901, that moment appeared imminent. On May 29, Helen signed a title bond with W.H. Bancroft, representing Harriman's Oregon Short Line Railroad, for $65,000, well above her original asking price of $55,000. She received $500 in earnest money, with $5,000 to be paid by June 15 and the remainder in July. For reasons never explained but readily inferred from events, the railroad failed to pay, thus forfeiting their option on the ranch. Helen waited, aware that her assets would be essential to a southern railroad route. In August, 1901, apparently responding to a request from a Clark surveyor, she described the assets of the ranch and the provisions of the defunct Oregon Short Line deal. The surveyor's enthusiastic report to the Clarks in January, 1902, signaled serious interest.[3]

Meanwhile, both railroads were building southward, with the two titans locked in battle, in the courts, in appeals to various government authorities, and on the ground between opposing railroad crews armed with shovels. In September 1901, as railroad historian David Myrick has written, both crews were near Caliente "grading down the Meadow Valley Wash with a vengeance." Then, abruptly in mid-November, all activity stopped. Far from the public eye, the warring parties had declared a truce. This resulted in a compromise in July 1902 that established joint Harriman-Clark ownership of the southern route, to be named the San Pedro, Los Angeles, and Salt Lake with Clark holding control. Clark could now proceed with the purchase of the Las Vegas Ranch.[4]

In October 1902, Helen journeyed to Salt Lake City for her momentous meeting with William Clark. Apparently they got along very well. He later wrote admiringly to her "if any one deserves the honor attached to the name of pioneer and credit for attracting the attention of capitalists to that country, you certainly do ..." Perhaps her experience in this remote desert outpost reminded him of his own early days in the West. They signed a preliminary deal for $55,000, with a $5,000 down payment. Under the provisions of this agreement, the Stewarts would turn over their herd of five hundred cattle to Clark, retaining fifty head for themselves, as well as their herd of 150 horses. Helen would also keep the "Four Acres" tract, with a right to four inches of water from the creek for irrigation. Although the amount of cultivated land on the ranch was stated, Helen verbally estimated the flow of water from the creek and springs at 440 inches. If the agreement became final, the Stewarts would vacate the ranch in April, 1903, turning over all personal property to Clark.[5]

During the intervening months, a Clark agent, William McDermott, would inventory the property, and William Clark's younger brother, J. Ross Clark, would deal with day-to-day matters. This period proved contentious because McDermott found much to criticize and the tall, thin J. Ross Clark, eleven years younger than William and living in Los Angeles, proved to be a like-minded micromanager (their exchanges were part of the Union Pacific papers serendipitously saved from the Yermo dump in southern

California and acquired by the University of Nevada Las Vegas). The root of McDermott's difficulties appeared to be that the Stewarts' evaluation of their holdings had been based on estimates and an old U.S. survey that proved inaccurate, while McDermott wanted exact figures and seized upon every discrepancy.[6]

Trouble erupted from the start. When McDermott and Hira rode out to see the cattle, McDermott found that the entire herd had not been gathered together in the pasture. "I showed my displeasure in an unmistakable manner, which had a good effect ..." he wrote to Clark attorney Charles O. Whittemore. Similarly, he found the horses small, wild, and insufficient in number, understandably refusing to include unbroken mustangs in the count. Every object, no bush or shovel excluded, received his disapproving scrutiny. Some mesquite fence posts had rotted at the base; the peach orchard appeared overgrown; the survey of the "Four Acres" graveyard, to be withheld by the Stewarts, placed it too close to the creek; and on and on. The principal shortcomings he dwelled upon were the flow of water in the spring and creek (less than Helen had verbally estimated) and the acreage suitable for farming (also less than represented). In mid-November, on J. Ross Clark's suggestion, McDermott made a "bold proposition" to wring concessions from Helen: the Stewarts should give up all stock with none reserved and all hay. He would make exceptions for immediate needs: a team, two or three saddle horses, and enough hay for the winter. He also would like the graves in the "Four Acres" moved.[7]

McDermott's derogatory evaluation of the ranch clearly aroused resentment among the Stewarts. After all, it had been their home, their living, and a source of pride to them for twenty years. McDermott complained to J. Ross that "Old Lady Stewart" (Helen was then forty-eight) had been "kicking pretty hard" against the concessions in his bold proposition. Finding the family "hard people to deal with," he attempted to enlist Frank Stewart's influence on the "old lady," an indication that Helen's affection for Frank was even evident to an outsider. It is notable that of the many people who came in contact with Helen and commented on her, only McDermott viewed her unpleasantly.[8]

When not kicking back against McDermott, the old lady mainly concerned herself with securing titles to the lands she had purchased in addition to the original ranch. Soon she accomplished this, as her land purchases had been duly recorded in the county recorder's office in Pioche. An investigation by Clark's attorney confirmed that all were in order. In McDermott's supplementary report on the property, the final cattle count of about five hundred conformed to the contract; the horse count fell far short.[9]

Perhaps for this reason, Helen yielded. Although she moved no graves, she agreed to a new description of the "Four Acres" area separating it from the creek as McDermott wished, and she gave up all the Stewart stock, including the reserved fifty head of cattle that would have enabled them to continue ranching on a small scale nearby. Several months later, McDermott refused Hira's attempt to buy back fifty head. When Hira expressed an intention to buy them elsewhere and run them on the open range, McDermott acidly observed to J. Ross Clark that Hira was likely to brand cattle not his own. "However whisky may step in & be our friend in this matter & unfit him for the task." It is reasonable to suppose that Hira took the loss of the ranch very hard and had not accepted the end of his life as a stockman.[10]

In mid-December, Helen set out to see Eva. By this time, Eva had married James Coffey and moved to San Francisco. The Clarks wanted the signatures of all the children on the deed reaffirming that they had turned over their interests in the ranch to their mother. Eva posed no problem. The problem had been Hira, who had balked at signing. He seemed to cling to a golden age in which the Stewarts lived forever on the ranch that had been his boyhood home and his widowed mother never remarried. Pressured by his siblings, he finally signed the deed.[11]

Helen continued her journey to Salt Lake City, ready to submit the deed, backdated to December 8, and revised to reflect the concessions she had made. William Clark received advice generally in favor of purchasing the ranch. Surveyor John T. McWilliams thought that despite the deficiencies the property was "worth the price to a railroad company." Even McDermott, after initially urging against purchase unless the Stewarts made concessions, two weeks later pronounced himself satisfied with all but the water and favored closing the deal. The sole dissenter was J. Ross Clark, who thought the Stewarts "a hard lot" and foresaw "a good deal of trouble" settling the sale. He advised his brother not to settle as planned because Helen had misrepresented the farm land and water.[12]

The most soundly reasoned advice came from Clark's attorney, Charles O. Whittemore. He pointed out that the ranch land comprised 1,840 acres, Helen having nearly doubled the original 960 acres by her purchases. All were legally in order. Helen had declared that 320 acres had been cultivated and the flow of water on the ranch was

440 inches (a critical matter in arid Nevada); McDermott claimed 200 inches of water flow and less than 100 cultivated acres, figures that Helen heartily disputed. Whittemore observed that the Stewarts held "absolute" water rights to all the springs inside the tract. He added that a long continued drought and a seasonal decrease in flow probably accounted for the disparity between Helen's verbal estimate and McDermott's. He pointed out that if Clark decided to "disaffirm the sale," it would "probably mean litigation" by the Stewarts and a "risk" of losing the place to other buyers instead of a reduction in price. Even if McDermott's figures on water and cultivated land proved correct, "I still believe the property is worth more than you have contracted to pay for it, if its importance to the railroad is considered."[13]

William Clark was a man for the big picture. Not for him to quibble over rotten mesquite fence posts or cultivated acreage. He was the "Montana Midas," conservatively estimated to be worth $100,000,000 in the days when a million was still worth something, and undoubtedly he was mulling over a prosperous roundhouse town for his railroad, not a ranch. Whittemore was right: for the land and water, the ranch merited Helen's price. Yet he long postponed his decision. At the end of December, he still had not accepted the deed. On February 26, and perhaps earlier, Helen was staying with her old friend Mary Carman, who had moved to Salt Lake City from Pioche. It is not unlikely that Helen's presence reflected an effort to influence the outcome of the sale by positioning herself near Clark's influential attorney, Whittemore.[14]

This interregnum period must have been a suspenseful one for the Stewarts, as well as others involved, because they had no way of knowing whether William Clark would proceed with the sale as planned, bargain for a lower price, or drop the sale entirely as the OSL had done. During this trying time, Helen's interests were ably represented by her attorney, Frank R. McNamee, or, as she addressed him, "kind friend." The Stewarts and McNamees remained warm friends for years, even after Frank moved to Los Angeles and became an employee of the railroad. At the ranch, Will, uncertain of the future, went ahead with the necessary routines, seeding, pruning, and spring plowing. At the same time, he began building a small house for Helen, Lena, and himself on the "Four Acres." At times, Will and Lena were the only Stewarts still present on the ranch. To requests for ranching supplies from McDermott, J. Ross Clark replied that his brother's plans remained unknown.[15]

*A gathering at the wall (early 1903). Left to right: Frank, Will, Helen, Eva, Hira, and Tiza.*
*UNLV Special Collections*

Having won his points by Helen's concessions, McDermott was temporarily at peace with the Stewarts and observed that they had been "very kind," while maintaining a constant barrage of criticism about ranching practices he considered negligent. He vented the worst of his spleen at other targets: first at McWilliams, whose bill for surveying the ranch he considered "outrageous"; later at George Lattimer, leasee at the Kiel ranch, whom he suspected of selling liquor to Indians. In 1901, the Harriman interests had bought the 240-acre place from the Georges for a fire sale price of $6,500, subsequently turning it over to the combined railroad. Discord with J. Ross Clark over the charges for Will's work continued for some time. The suspense ended when it was announced that the Stewarts would leave the ranch within ten days. Without any dickering over the price, Clark made known his decision and finalized the deal.[16]

After a final heated argument between Will and McDermott, the Stewarts vacated the ranch by April, as promised. In another April, a very reluctant young wife had arrived there, expecting to remain only a year or two. There she had buried her "beloved husband and only friend" after his murder. There she had stayed ever since, managing a large agricultural enterprise and making it even larger through her investments, raising five children alone, and becoming the well-known mistress of the Mormon Trail. There she had buried her adored youngest son. Now, twenty-one years after that first April, she had left the Las Vegas Ranch forever. It was the end of an era.

Helen went to spend a while in Los Angeles, as did her sons and their families. It is reasonable to suppose that Frank Stewart was also present, staying with his brother,

HELEN J. STEWART: FIRST LADY OF LAS VEGAS

Madison. Frank may have appeared to be an employee, but he had larger prospects in view. Although it is a matter of conjecture, possibly around this time, or a little earlier in the year, Helen made known her intention to marry Frank. From Hira, still clinging to the golden age and smarting from the loss of the ranch, the reaction was negative. Helen took him seriously.[17]

*A visit to Sutro Heights, San Franciso. From left: Frank,*
*Helen, Leslie, Dreeme, and two of Dreme's sisters.*
*Nevada State Museum Las Vegas*

CHAPTER 6: THE END OF AN ERA

She did nothing. Then Hira went swimming in the chilly and unfamiliar waters of the Pacific. He caught a cold that developed into pneumonia and died unexpectedly on June 19 at the age of twenty-nine. He left a widow, Dreeme, and two small children, Leslie, a toddler of four, and Geneva, an infant born in 1900. His body was embalmed in a mausoleum pending future burial in the "Four Acres."[18]

Helen did not mourn her second son's death for long. She had Frank sign a prenuptial agreement, at a time when such agreements remained unusual and frontier women had recently been struggling for the right to influence domestic decisions such as purchasing a sewing machine. Not Helen. The agreement gave her complete control of all wealth and property she possessed at the time of the marriage. Under no circumstances would she have jeopardized her children's inheritance. On July 21, barely a month after Hira's death, she married Frank in the Methodist Episcopal Church in Ventura. The timing clearly signalled that only Hira had delayed their union.

Around Las Vegas a legend later went the rounds that Helen had married Frank in preference to other suitors because she would not be obliged to change her last name. It seems the source was one of Helen's rejected admirers, John Powers, an early prospecter in El Dorado. After the sale of his best mine, the Wall Street, for a considerable sum in 1898, he decided that he might now be worthy of Helen's hand and proposed to her. Helen replied, "You are a fine man, John, but I won't change my name." Although her marriage to a man named Stewart five years later gave plausibility to this legend, it is unlikely that she intended to marry Frank as early as 1898. Perhaps she merely gave an excuse to sooth Powers's bruised feelings. To marry

HELEN J. STEWART: FIRST LADY OF LAS VEGAS

just for the sake of a name would have been a form of frivolity alien to Helen. All the same, this bit of folklore survived because Las Vegans who became acquainted with Frank socially could think of no other reason for Helen's marital choice.[19]

The family was evolving in other new directions. Delia had made herself into a successful business woman, owning and operating a water works in Galt at a time when few women engaged in businesses unconnected to domestic activities. Also, in her late sixties, she married a man named John Goldsworthy in Los Angeles. Apparently the relationship did not last long because subsequent sources on Delia do not mention Goldsworthy. Unfortunately, no communications between Delia and the Stewarts survive from this period. If Delia's activities aroused no comment, Eva's offered more fuel for talk. While still in her teens, Eva had married a man whose business was horse racing. James Coffey, called Jimmy, stabled his horses in Oakland, and the couple lived in San Francisco, when not off to the races at the heart of the sporting life.[20]

Even without Hira, Will showed signs of reentering the cattle business on a small scale. Earlier in the year, Helen had bought 280 acres, forty of it north of the "Four Acres" and adjacent to it and the remainder in a strip extending eastward. In late June, she ordered enough barbed wire to fence six and one-half miles of land. Will bought some cattle in September and the next month asked Walter Bracken, McDermott's more tolerant replacement as "boss" of the Las Vegas Ranch, if he might buy seventeen head from the ranch herd. Requesting permission from J. Ross Clark, Bracken observed that this would make no difference because Will had already accumulated a small herd from other sellers. Predictably, J. Ross Clark's reaction was sharply negative. He ordered Bracken to sell no cattle to Will and dispose of the herd otherwise. Time would show, however, that Will's future would take a different course than cattle ranching.[21]

With plenty of money, a new husband, and the world at her feet, Helen moved back to Las Vegas in the autumn of 1903 into the modest house that Will, reliable Will, had built for them north of the "Four Acres" and across the street — if street is the appropriate word — from the Las Vegas Ranch. The time Helen foretold to her children when civilization would come to the Las Vegas Valley had not yet arrived. No church spires, no smoke from puffing trains, and no community of nice houses. The San Pedro, Los Angeles, and Salt Lake Railroad still had not reached the Las Vegas Ranch, and its northern and southern ends would not be joined until 1905 at Jean, Nevada, twenty-three miles to the south.[22] Indistinct as a mirage, Las Vegas was still taking shape, less a town than an idea. All the same, this place that Helen had so strongly resisted on her arrival had become home over the years. When she could have gone anywhere, Helen returned to Las Vegas.

# Chapter 7: *First Lady of Las Vegas*

While Las Vegas developed into an actual town, Helen J. Stewart became the pioneer icon. At the outset, she would see the transformation of her former ranch and the resolution of several conflicts. No longer would circumstances oblige her to be one of the combatants and "kick back." She could simply observe as an investor and an historian of the Las Vegas Valley without being bruised as the Clarks ruthlessly vanquished all competitors. J. Ross Clark's refusal to provide needed supplies to the ranch despite the requests of McDermott and Bracken had long presaged another future for the place. This became obvious in the fall of 1903 when J. Ross Clark ordered Bracken to dispose of the ranch herd of some five hundred cattle (though not to the Stewarts). The announcement by the Clarks that Las Vegas would be the location for the railroad's roundhouse, a large circular building for housing and repairing engines, made it official. Las Vegas was going to be a railroad town.[1]

As the railroad built steadily southward, with a new tent camp forming at each stopping place, John McWilliams saw an opportunity. Having bought some acreage from Helen on the west side of the proposed tracks, the red-haired Canadian-born surveyor conceived a bold plan. He would develop the town he advertised as "The Original Las Vegas" while the Clarks lingered at the starting gate. The "Original Las Vegas" was an instant hit, boosted by rumored gold discoveries at Bullfrog ninety miles south of Goldfield in the summer of 1904. After the railroad reached the Las Vegas Ranch in October, many freighters made the McWilliams town their base to capitalize on the magnified traffic northwest toward Bullfrog and the central Nevada mining boom. McWilliams sold lots for low prices, some 150 of them. The "Original Las Vegas" emerged as a conglomeration of white tents and tent cabins, with a few more substantial buildings scattered among them. Saloons predominated.[2]

Despite her many years on the frontier, Helen had never witnessed a transportation boom. Silver Mountain had been a minor excitement; Pioche had already started to decline by the time she moved there. Now she would see one in progress. Day and night "a steady procession of eight- to twenty-animal teams drawing high-wheeled freight wagons each loaded with immense quantities of supplies and equipment ... struck out for Bullfrog and adjacent camps," writes Stanley Paher. "As many as fifty freighters daily passed each other on the Las Vegas-Bullfrog run." These contributed to the billowing clouds of dust raised by local teams laden with supplies for the building boom as they churned through the streets in all directions.[3]

The Clarks may have been slower than McWilliams at townsite development, but when they began, they roared forward with the inexorable force of a juggernaut. East of the tracks, they neatly platted the streets and blocks of "Clark's Las Vegas Townsite," as they advertised it. At the insistence of the Union Pacific, they switched from direct sales of lots to an auction before an excited and tumultuous crowd on May 15, 1905. Some two hundred avid investors had taken the Salt Lake train from Los Angeles to vie for the best locations.[4]

The depopulation of the "Original Las Vegas" followed, as drays hauled tent houses, primitive hotels, and stores to the Clark site. Within weeks the first Las Vegas, where several minor fires had broken out, looked pitifully forlorn, but it still clung to life. A few cafes, stables, and stores served the traffic bound for the boom towns, and southbound stages disgorged their passengers at this point.[5]

McWilliams, however, had one compensation. During that May, he watched with intense pleasure while the Clarks began building an ice house, unaware that the small scrap of land east of the tracks and north of their townsite that they had chosen belonged to McWilliams, part of his land purchase from Helen. He let them build, then demonstrated that the land belonged to him and presented them with a $5,000 bill for the property. Now primarily responsible for the railroad while his brother occupied himself with more momentous matters, J. Ross Clark was enraged at McWilliams for failing to raise the matter sooner and at his own engineers. The Clarks abandoned $10,000 worth of construction, started the ice plant anew farther south, and refused to pay McWilliams. Nonetheless, McWilliams and his wife had more staying power than many who came and went during those frantic years. For the rest of their lives, they remained in the Las Vegas home he had built for them.[6]

No doubt Helen felt relieved that she now had few dealings with the railroad, as she watched the Clarks swat McWilliams like a fly and drive out a more formidable challenger to their control, millionaire Francis M. "Borax" Smith. After incorporating the Tonopah and Tidewater Railroad, Smith believed the Clarks had assured him that his railroad could extend northwest from Las Vegas and commenced construction. Meanwhile, the Clarks decided that they wanted to dominate transportation in the region of the central Nevada mining boom with a railroad of their own. By denying use of their tracks to Smith and allowing him no freight discounts, they drove Smith out of Las Vegas, but he proved no less tenacious than McWilliams. At Ludlow, California, a solid agreement with the Santa Fe Railroad allowed him to build his Tonopah and Tidewater. Meanwhile, the Clarks bought the equipment and track he had already built for a separate railroad of their own to be called the Las Vegas and Tonopah. It would reach Rhyolite in December, 1906, shortly before the boom collapsed. At the same time, a third railroad, the Bullfrog and Goldfield, began building south from Goldfield. Smith would acquire it in 1908 as part of his line. As the boom towns withered, two railroads from the south began to seem an expensive luxury.[7]

For years, railroads would be the backbone of the Las Vegas economy. With a permanent force of roundhouse workers, the San Pedro, Los Angeles, and Salt Lake Railroad remained the town's largest employer, but as Ralph Roske points out, a series of natural disasters of near biblical proportions caused "severe economic troubles." These began with a train wreck and minor floods in 1905 and continued in February 1907 when a storm washed out roads and bridges north of Las Vegas in the Meadow Valley Wash, halting rail service for over a month. Repairs were expensive because raising the level of the tracks, altering stream channels, and erecting eight steel bridges occupied seven hundred workers and cost three-quarters of a million dollars. An even worse catastrophe struck in the great flood of 1910 that wrecked over one hundred miles of track and rolling stock, mainly in the Meadow Valley Wash and Clover Valley. A train that reached Las Vegas at the end of December would not arrive in Salt Lake City until

HELEN J. STEWART: FIRST LADY OF LAS VEGAS

June. Although they investigated other routes, the Clarks decided to keep the existing route, whatever the expense.[8]

The summer of 1905 that followed the Clark auction was afterward remembered as the hottest and windiest ever. It may have led some who had contested fiercely for lots to question their judgment. Wives less intrepid than Helen decamped in such numbers that the editor of the new *Las Vegas Age* worried that Las Vegas would not develop into a town with established homes. This concern proved needless. In cooler weather the wives returned, and nearly half the adults in 1910 were married. This differed from the early stages in a mining camp, when characteristically the boomers were young, male, and single. While the summer heat lasted, the Las Vegas Ranch, with its welcoming shade trees became a place of rest and refreshment for those fleeing the new towns, where not a tree nor a blade of grass had yet grown. Realizing that their charges could not survive confinement in such heat, officers gave their prisoners a special dispensation: deputies chained them to the tree roots, shifting their position with the angle of the sun.[9]

During the early years, this railroad town, its fortunes fluctuating with the storm clouds over the Meadow Valley Wash, remained far from the city of Helen's vision. There had been improvements: a water system, several oiled streets and curbing, more nice homes, and somewhat unreliable electricity. Nonetheless, those who walked the streets at night carried lanterns, and such niceties as a long-planned sewer system and garbage collection arrived only slowly. Because the church spires of Helen's vision appeared tardily, she attended to the Episcopalians herself and played an important role in the founding of Christ

Church in 1907. When the Episcopal Ladies Guild was organized in the fall of 1907, the rector, Reverend Harry Gray, asked the women to name the church. They chose Christ Church, which Helen may have suggested remembering her connections to Christ Church in Pioche. The number of small farms springing up around the valley heartened Helen because it fostered her hope that the settlement might become a more normal community. Helen had grown up on farms and ranched all her adult life. Farms meant normalcy to her. In her writings, she praised the Las Vegas Valley as an agricultural paradise, extolling the apples "of a superior size and quality," the excellence of the grape vines brought from France and Spain, the opportunities for raising cattle on the wild grasses abounding in the region, and much more.[10]

*Early photo of Las Vegas showing the Methodist church (left)*
*and the Episcopal church (right). ca 1908*
*Ed Von Tobel*

Despite the end of the central Nevada mining boom, some latecomers still dreamed the old dream. In 1906 William Clark confided to Helen that he was considering visiting Bullfrog himself. Although she had never done so before 1900, Helen extended her investments to mines, probably drawn by the interest of Will and Frank, who reportedly had a background in mining before he came to work at the ranch. The golden opportunity was rapidly passing, however. Its pay dirt depleted, Rhyolite busted in 1907 to become a spectacular ghost town. After mine owner George Wingfield and U.S. troops broke the backs of the radical labor unions in 1907, Goldfield declined into a quiet company town by 1910, losing some two-thirds of the people who had crowded its streets in palmier days; and Tonopah had morphed from a field of dreams into a stable mining town like many another. Yet, for some, hope sprang eternal. Josephine and George Scott, two novice prospectors from California, reported that prospectors still flooded Las Vegas in 1914. These, however, were not permanent residents. The census taker could find only 945 people there in 1910. Reliable employment by the railroad made Las Vegas a more stable town, with families and a slightly older population, than the volatile mining camps. The place remained in essence what it had been since 1905 — a core of railroad workers and a horde of transient prospectors headed into the desert.[11]

Having resigned as postmaster on leaving the ranch, Helen held no official position. Nonetheless, she was becoming the first historian of southern Nevada, and for good reason: like Ishmael in Herman Melville's *Moby Dick*, she was the last one left to tell the tale. The Gass family had moved away, the Kiels had died, two of them violently, Jim

Wilson had succumbed to the infirmities of old age in 1906, and George Allen was gone as well. An attorney's letter to her seeking information on the Kiels illustrated her place as the source people consulted when a question on the history of the Las Vegas Valley arose. Historian was a role that Helen took seriously, writing to Mormon authorities for an accurate accounting of the Mormon mission in the valley before her arrival. It was also a role that she obviously enjoyed, speaking before clubs and other groups on the subject and regaling newcomers with tidbits of local history. She accepted Carson City newspaperman Sam Davis's invitation to write a chapter on the early history of the valley in his 1913 two volume history of Nevada.

In "Early Knowledge of Nevada," the article Helen wrote in Davis' *History of Nevada*, Helen begins by giving considerable attention to the short eighteenth century visit to the area by the Franciscan fathers. Over the ensuing centuries, the Southern Paiutes continued to use the limited Spanish taught them by the padres and to revere their religious teachings. Their "crumbling forts and abandoned mines" still remained in Helen's time, and many "interesting relics," such as Spanish coins and a rosary, testified to their visit. Helen then briefly covers the "trappers and traders" and the failed Mormon colony. Ever an advocate of agricultural efforts, she sympathized with the Moapa Valley Mormons when taxation problems compelled them to abandon their farms, but she skips rather lightly over Octavious Gass.

The shocker, to anyone who still remembered, came almost at the end of her article. Helen declares: "This goodly sum of money accumulating at the ranch [from sales to El Dorado] soon attracted the attention of a band of robbers, headed by a man named Hank Parish. They soon matured a plan whereby they thought to come easily and quickly into possession of a couple of thousand dollars of this hard-earned cash. They also arranged to ... steal a valuable band of horses to carry them out of the country. Choosing their time they waylaid and attacked Mr. Stewart, killing and robbing him. They then separated and took flight, some into California, some into Arizona, and one of them into Utah."

This, of course, was false, as to the robbery, the band of thieves, and their escape to three different states. Although nearly thirty years had passed since Archie's murder, Helen could hardly have forgotten the circumstances. It seemed likely that a false memory had taken hold, as sometimes happens after a traumatic event, and that Helen believed it herself. The explanation of robbery may have been fostered by a guilty sense that her very vocal distress over Henry's harassment may have driven Archie to his death. Helen's article closes with a gracious acknowledgement of the important help in caring for the ranch that her father gave after Archie's death.[12]

Recognizing her place as the valley's first historian, people brought her artifacts relating to the Spanish presence in the area, to add to her already fabled collection of Indian basketry. When the city of Las Vegas was incorporated, the silver pen that the governor used to sign the bill was given to Helen by newspaperman Charles P. Squires. Helen's collaboration with Jeanne Wier provided further proof of her place as a historian, as well as a history maker in her own right. Director for forty-five years of the historical society that she founded in 1904 and professor for forty-one years at the University of Nevada, Wier dominated state history and jealously guarded her turf. When she journeyed to Las Vegas in the summer of 1908, she visited Helen and soon decided that a branch of the Nevada Historical Society should be organized in Las Vegas. Who better to do it than Helen? And who else would be chosen its first president? Because Wier was a thorny personality who sometimes turned against other historians, her admiration for Helen probably contributed to their friendly and lasting relationship. Wier wrote in her diary, "Truly she is a pioneer of the pioneers."[13]

This was how Las Vegans saw Helen. She was the pioneer icon, the widow who steadfastly persevered through hardship and danger in a remote and lonely place, the ministering angel who aided travelers on the Mormon trail, the inspiration who held to a vision of the town Las Vegas would become, even when it seemed most unlikely. Many who had made a good deal of money in mining from the Comstock to Goldfield vamoosed to build a luxurious home in California. Not Helen. She stayed in Las Vegas, living among the townspeople in the modest little house Will had built for her after she left the ranch. There she became the community builder whose many civic activities helped develop Las Vegas beyond its raw beginnings. This was the Helen they knew — and revered.

No aspect of the valley's past fascinated Helen more than the role of the Southern Paiutes. She assiduously pursued Indian myths, language, and stories, perhaps with a view toward the book that she hoped to write one day. She recognized the artistry in the beautiful baskets she collected, some purchased and some gifts to her from Indian friends. For years she had been much concerned with Southern Paiute welfare, offering them employment so that they might share in the bounty of the ranch and

HELEN J. STEWART: FIRST LADY OF LAS VEGAS

ministering to them when they became ill. Although her circumstances had changed, her concern had not, nor had their esteem for her. In 1912, she decided to sell the Indian Bureau a ten-acre tract of land to be a reservation for them where they could build homes and the children could attend an Indian school. (Reservation was the term used in this period; today a small enclave is called an Indian colony.) Helen's belief in the value of education had never lessened. Notably, this was not the sort of poor, desolate, and unworkable land to which Indians were usually relegated throughout the country, but a fine tract, with several springs, adjacent to the property where Helen herself resided. In fact, at a time when the valley's water table was high, the new small farms depended on wells, as did Helen herself after problems developed over the allotment from the creek that had been promised to her.[14]

With a shove from Nevada congressman Ed Roberts, the Indian Bureau agreed to "provide a permanent home for the wanderers," and the deed transferring the property from Helen to the tribe was recorded in 1912, though the reservation did not become a reality for several years. The *Age* saw its proximity to Helen's own property as positive. "Mrs. Stewart has always been a good friend to the Indians and it is very desirable that their permanent home should be so located as to bring them within her influence and control." The subtext of the need for Helen's influence and control may have been the mistrust of Indians that lingered from the panic over Mouse, the terror aroused by the much more dangerous and recent Indian murderer Queho, and a general public unease over the presence of Indians among them.[15]

At moments Helen may have wished for greater influence

and control over her own family, especially the members that deviated from the paths she would have preferred. The sources are fragmentary because Will, Frank, and Eva (who returned to Las Vegas) were all present and communications with them were verbal. On Tiza the sources are more extensive because she traveled widely and saved her correspondence. Evelyn Moden, Helen's grandaughter, loaned the letters to Carrie Townley Porter and subsequently donated them to the Nevada Historical Society in Reno. The Helen J. Stewart Collection was later transferred to the Nevada State Museum Las Vegas.

Helen's main worry in this period was Tiza. Although Tiza secured an elementary school teacher's certificate in 1903, she apparently did not settle down to teach. Rather, she married Charles A. Rucker, nine years older than she. He was a doctor who had graduated from Barnes Medical College in St. Louis and advertised himself as a specialist in surgery and "diseases of women and children." The exact date of their marriage has not come to light, but it must have been between August, 1904 (the last reference to Tiza Stewart) and November, 1905 (the first reference to her as Mrs. C.A. Rucker). The ceremony likely took place in Los Angeles, where Tiza frequently spent time. Items on patients Rucker treated, more often successfully than not, regularly appeared in the press. Medical skill and close attendance could not, however, save Jim Wilson during the old pioneer's last months of life (and Rucker did not hesitate to remind Wilson to kindly attend to his bill "at once"). Years later Sheriff Sam Gay reminisced about Rucker's exceptional skill as a surgeon. The doctor had sewn up a severe gash in the sheriff's head so cleverly that it left no scar, as well as repairing several other men.

When Helen developed pneumonia with complications in December, 1905, she recovered under Rucker's treatment. So, too, did the doctor's own wife following an accident. In May, 1907, Tiza and Helen were riding in a buckboard when the horse, an imperfectly broken mustang, bolted. Difficult as it is to imagine, Helen, though hampered by her long skirts, leapt with alacrity out of the rig, but when the horse crashed into the fence, Tiza was thrown from her seat and suffered severe injuries, an arm broken above and below the elbow, a leg broken above the ankle, and a long gash across her forehead. Yet cared for by her husband and tenderly nursed in her mother's home, she was pronounced "wholly recovered" in only eight weeks.[16]

Tiza had borne her injuries "philosophically," having already gone through a greater tragedy. As her husband hastened to join her in Los Angeles, she gave birth to twin girls in the last week of August, 1906, but sadly they lived only a day or two. The babies were wrapped in their little blankets and placed with Hira in his coffin at the mausoleum in Los Angeles. In May of 1908, Will brought Hira and the twins home to Las Vegas for burial in the "Four Acres" family cemetery.[17]

Later that year, Tiza and the doctor apparently agreed to go their separate ways, and Tiza's restless travels began, as did Helen's effort to persuade her to return to Las Vegas and divorce Rucker. In a revealing letter of October 8 to Tiza in Salt Lake City, Helen wrote: "Enclosed is a letter from his 'Nibs' One might sing to his music in three or four different tunes. Do not pay any attention to anything like a threat. I think for awhile the best thing is to keep entirely out of his way. He will get tired of trying to be smart and decide to go somewhere himself and when he gets tired of floundering around and if you decide you cannot live with him just come right here and you can get a Divorce just as easily and quickly as any where else. His drunkenness just before leaving here is more against him than any thing his fertile brain can make up against you. So when you are ready come to me and if you wish it we will fight it out together against him if it must be so write me immediately just what we will do I am at your command for any thing for your good. Do not leave Salt Lake to go any farther East at this time of year it is too cold."[18]

Tiza rejected every aspect of her mother's advice. She must have firmly discarded the idea of divorce, which Helen's subsequent letters do not mention. In fact, the Ruckers would not divorce in Helen's lifetime. If this does not indicate lingering affection, it certainly shows that neither wanted to marry someone else. Rucker had, however, left Las Vegas for parts unknown, presumably liberated from the annoyance of phonographs. In a 1907 column in the *Age* on "Things citizens are thankful for," Rucker's item read: "For strength to withstand the phonographs that harass my nerves by day and haunt my sleep at night."[19]

Far from returning to Las Vegas, Tiza headed east, writing from Red Cloud, Nebraska. She visited relatives never previously met, including Delia's sister Angeline. They had stayed behind in the Midwest when Delia, Hiram, and their children embarked on the momentous journey to California. Quite forgetting that Tiza was now a capable young woman of thirty experienced with independent living during her sojourn in Los Angeles with her younger siblings, Helen clucked over her "Darling Girlie" like a mother hen. "Keep warm. Dont take any chances," she urged Tiza in a February letter. "Aunt Angeline and the folks will know when the

HELEN J. STEWART: FIRST LADY OF LAS VEGAS

Storms are dangerous ... The papers are full of the Cold Blizzards in the East. I do hope you will not undertake much travel during this very cold period Among so many of the relatives there will surely be some safe resting place during the stormy period which is liable to be from now on until the 1st of April." As a child, Helen had known the midwestern winters. She closed her letter with "enjoy yourself all you can and above all keep warm."[20]

In an April letter, Helen sounded more resigned to Tiza's wanderings, at least for the moment. "Poor little girl it is too bad for you to be so far from home. I wish things were sweeter in life for you If you only have your health and can keep out of ... cyclones and Blizzards and I can get to see you sometime when you are through sight seeing I will be a happy Mamma. All is not happiness ... so I will abide in Patience ..." Helen added a little enticement with comments on the large rise in Las Vegas property values. Helen would know because she continued to dabble in real estate and had become a landlady with several houses for rent. Her drive to acquire as much land as possible had slackened, however, after the sale to the railroad brought a large sum to the Stewarts and she no longer worried about providing for her children's future.[21]

By late June, as Tiza's travels continued, Helen's pleas for her return grew more pitiful. She had Will, Frank, and Eva close at hand, but she wanted her eldest daughter, her confidante, the one to whom she had opened her heart after little Archie's tragic death. She wanted Tiza. "Time silence and absence are pitiless destructives," she wrote, "Do not let these tear down the structure that has grown with your birth and my being. Your loving Mother. I am so lonely to see you this morning. The wind seems to be coming in with a lonely sigh. All Nature seems joining in the cry come back, come home to those that love you. Eva and I are makin aprons the kind you wore before leaving here ... I wish you were here with us." Helen's anxieties over the weather switched from the cold of winter to the heat of summer. "I dread you going into the warm humid atmosphere of the cities of Chicago and New York-unless you take great precaution you will suffer-not being used to the weather. So many people of those cities die of heat prostration in the summer months." Evidently Helen failed to realize that not everyone thought the Las Vegas climate as salubrious as she did. Soon afterward bank correspondence shows that Helen had become concerned over Tiza's withdrawals.[22]

In a late August letter, Helen even offered Tiza what was, for her, the ultimate sacrifice — leaving Las Vegas. "Tiza come home and we will go into something here to make us a good living and be happy to be with each other ... Tiza do not stay in that storm swept country. Come home I am so lonesome to see you. And if you do not want to stay here any longer than a month or so we will go somewhere else awhile." Now concerned that Tiza might be short of funds, she offered to arrange banking matters so that her daughter would have money to draw on. All to no avail.[23]

By early September, Helen began to suspect that Tiza's sojourn in the Midwest signified a reconciliation with Rucker. "I sometimes think perhaps the Dr may be with you or near as Kansas City is his old home. When the Dr was sober no better Dr or better man to be found. But Drunk, just like all the other whiskey bedizened human beings. More beast than man education business love of Mother Wife offspring all gone. and the Mother might as

HELEN J. STEWART: FIRST LADY OF LAS VEGAS

well have no son. The wife as well no husband and children certainly are better off with no Father than such a one." Tiza continued her restless wanderings.[24]

Helen pled for her return no more. Her subsequent letters mainly conveyed family news. In 1914 (in her first typewritten letter), she added an account of a wealthy and powerful man whom Tiza might "set your Cap" for and a reminder that Las Vegas is a "good country to live in and a Good country to invest in."[25]

Indeed Helen had a good deal of family news to convey. While Tiza roamed, Eva had been in the midst of a crisis reported by Helen in her letters to Tiza. When racing his horses in Canada, Eva's husband, Jimmy Coffey, had suffered a severe head injury (perhaps in a fall from a horse). Although the doctor in the Victoria hospital where he lay did not expect him to live, his condition improved. Eva stayed with him in the hospital during his recovery, impatiently writing her mother that "the English are so slow." She anticipated a month or two more of hospital care, and the doctor warned that it would "not be good for Jimmy to be near a race track for a long time." Helen was sympathetic. "Poor Boy it is too bad I am so sorry. Such a faithful honest good man. The days cannot be all sunshine through our lives."[26]

How long Jimmy followed medical advice and stayed away from race tracks is not clear. In February 1909, Eva wrote that Jimmy and she were "doing farely well" and apparently so were his horses. Helen observed that the newspapers were full of the wonderful performance of Em and Em and their little jockey. Nonetheless, in the spring Jimmy unsuccessfully attempted to sell his horses in Albuquerque. He then raced them in Salt Lake City and contemplated Butte. His head injury continued to bother him a good deal. Meanwhile, Eva came home to Las Vegas to stay with Helen. "I am so glad she can stay," wrote Helen. "The wandring life of the Race Track seems to me so unsatisfactory." Jimmy eventually joined Eva. He briefly invested in a bakery, but clearly the ponies were more to his taste than the pies.[27]

*Eva, when she followed what Helen called*
*"the wandering life of the Rack Track" with*
*her first husband Jimmy (early 1909).*
*UNLV Special Collections*

Always first and foremost a mother, Helen gave up a much anticipated trip to Carson City as a delegate to the 1914 Federation of Women's Clubs conference, replete with entertainment by Governor Tasker Oddie and other "nice things," in order to care for Eva night and day when her daughter fell sick. This effort left Helen so tired that "it seemed I could never get rested," and she herself fell ill for two weeks. Nonetheless, with her usual stamina, she recovered. Her long-standing concern over following the races as an unsuitable way of life for Eva ended that spring when Eva filed for divorce and Jimmy left for the East. Helen commented: "It seems to me all the time that something is happening to make so much unhappiness ... [their divorce] seems a relief to me. It always seemed such a pity for a gentle character like Eva was as a girl to be placed by marriage where she was, as from a Moral standpoint there was nothing to be expected but destruction. It may be that with the help of some good man she may yet be able to adjust the conditions as to yet be very happy and get much good out of life. The things in life for her now are sure very distressing, and I am glad she is here where she can get the support of home." As it turned out, a different future for Eva was not so wild a dream.[28]

Even for Will, Helen's only surviving son and the rock of stability she had long relied on, the days were not "all sunshine," as Helen sometimes put it. Will had remained nearby in Las Vegas, and he developed into a civic leader after her own heart. He became captain of the firemen, ever an influential post in early western towns, and served on the Republican County Central Committee. When leading citizens organized a "Division Club" to press for splitting

Lincoln County, Will was on the committee to handle petitions to the legislature.

*Will, Helen's oldest child, whose birth she remembers as one of the "most wonderful events of my life."*
*Nevada State Museum Las Vegas*

The issue held no small importance to residents of southern Lincoln County because whenever someone wanted to file a mining claim or deal with county business, it meant a long trip to Pioche, even longer from Searchlight, El Dorado, and other settlements south of Las Vegas. The well-organized campaign by the Division Club won the day when Clark County, with Las Vegas the county seat, formally came into being after legislative approval on July 1, 1909, but at high cost (literally). The debt for the Pioche courthouse (in fact, closer to $600,000 than $1,000,000) remained unpaid, and the new county was obliged to assume $400,000 of it as the price of freedom.

Despite praise from the *Age* for his role in Las Vegas history — "The struggles, the hardships, the strenuous times that this family of pioneers experienced are history, and the candidate for long term commissioner is a part of that history ... In the conduct of the affairs of the great rancho he has gained a valuable business experience" — Will lost the election for long-term county commissioner to the Democratic candidate.[29]

Though called a "by profession a surveyor" and much in demand, Will served the county in a variety of ways: he was put in charge of the new road to El Dorado Canyon, a place he had known since boyhood when he accompanied his father on trips to sell beef and produce. A strong supporter of the movement to incorporate Las Vegas as a city, Will became the commissioner on streets and public property when the new city government was organized; the fiscal conservatism that led him to insist that county affairs be conducted on a "cash and carry" basis made him known as "the Watch Dog of the Treasury." Perhaps his most unusual service was "caging the birds," that is, accompanying the sheriff when two "bandits" and three other prisoners were escorted from the county jail to the state prison in Carson City.[30]

Will was also an investor, not only in mines but also in enterprises like the Charleston Hotel (named for the nearby mountain) that helped build Las Vegas into a real town. The new hotel, adobe on the first floor, including a bar and dining room, and frame on the second floor, with eleven rooms, was advertised as "cool and comfortable ... with a strictly first class bar." According to the *Clark County Review*, by 1911, Will and Helen together owned one-sixteenth of the land within the proposed Las Vegas city limits. All was not well for him at home, however. In September 1910 Helen wrote Eva and Jimmy that Will and Lena are deciding what to do.[31]

What they decided to do after seventeen years of a childless marriage, was divorce. Within a year of the divorce on June 22, 1912, both had remarried, Will to El Mina (called Mina) Hanson. Mina's name had been cropping up in Helen's correspondence for several years ("Is Mina still there?" for instance), but it was never clear whether Mina was a friend, a visitor, or an employee. Soon, in January 1913, she was there to stay as Will's second wife and on April 10, 1914, the mother of his only child. The couple named the baby Helen Jane after Will's mother.[32]

It was a difficult birth. Helen wrote Tiza: "it had to be taken with Instruments, which nearly cost the life of both The Mother and child, The baby is just finished relieving itself of the bruises on its poor little head, It was so hurt with the Instrument, it could not use its lower jaw to nurse for ten days, The nurse took the milk from the Mothers breast and fed it every two hours for ten days. It never cried until it was ten days old." As the baby gained weight, they were "feeling quite encouraged." Helen admired its "wonderful eyes, acts as if it knew many of the mysteries of life now." Nonetheless, it soon became clear that the baby was intellectually disabled. This made no difference to Helen. She adored the baby and delighted in every small advance the little one made. Helen had other grandchildren — Hira's offspring, Leslie and Geneva, now teenagers. Helen remained close to the Ganns and enjoyed their visits after Dreeme married Dr. Samuel Benson and bore another daughter. Will's baby was nonetheless a special child to Helen.[33]

During these years, Delia was aging and undergoing the common transition from caregiver to one in need of care, increasingly relying on her daughters. She spent a winter with Helen, as well as other visits, lived for a while with Flora, and sold her water works in Galt to Aseneth. With Rachel, Aseneth moved to the Galt farm, while Delia, when not staying with her daughters, moved to Los Angeles. Helen visited her there when she fell ill and wrote to Eva and Jimmy that her mother was "quite well." Having gained a reputation as the place to be, the Los Angeles population had burgeoned, leading Helen to observe: "Los Angeles is growing very fast — one would not recognize the old place we used to know. I would not like to live in the middle of the citys noise and confusion unless I was one of the large Merchants or Owner of a Block." Astute business woman though she was, Helen thought a large city bursting at the seams diverged too far from her ideal town.[34]

Of Frank, almost nothing is said in this period. Helen and he remained together and fond of each other, so far as we know. In Helen's many letters to Tiza, she lists her Christmas presents and often discusses the activities of friends, but only once does she mention Frank ("Frank sends his love"). Henry Lee, always a reliable observer of the Stewarts, recalled that he never saw any evidence of Frank "doing any work." Although never seen drunk (by Lee), Frank "sat around the wine cellar all day with these guys." Lee explained that this hangout was a rock structure to keep the wine cool built above ground a short distance from the house. Unlike Helen, Frank "acted like a man who wasn't much interested in anything. She was the dominant character, she was the stronger." Helen's friends did not regard him as a desirable dinner companion when he was "lit to the gills." In truth, Frank had become a kind of second-class husband. During an age when women generally were referred to — and referred to themselves — by the first names of their husbands (for instance, Mrs. James Givens), Helen proudly remained Mrs. Helen J. Stewart.[35]

So she appears on the membership roster of the Mesquite Club, an influential civic organization she helped found in 1911. Indeed, she had suggested the name and provided the club with a mesquite wood gavel that long remained in use. Delphine Squires recalled that when Helen proposed naming the first women's club in Las Vegas the Mesquite she said: "If the club could ever mean as much to the women of this community as the Mesquite tree had to the Indian women here on the desert we could not ask for more. They lived beneath the tree, cooked their food with its wood, made a liquor and also bread from the beans and sewed together the skins for their clothing with spines from the Mesquite."

This was a high level of aspiration for the Mesquite Club, but the members did more than socialize. They vigorously threw themselves into the activities that help to build a community. With Helen in charge, they raised money for planting some 2,000 trees in their dusty, treeless, shadeless town. After the planting on Arbor Day in 1912, they nurtured the young saplings, even when it meant toting buckets of water to them. Not least among their many activities, the Mesquite Club undertook numerous projects to fund the first public library in Las Vegas. Helen often spoke before the club in her usual pleasing manner, often on Indian legends or the interpretation of the baskets in her collection. She also brought these subjects to a wider audience when serving as delegate and guest of honor to the Nevada Federation of Women's Clubs in 1915.[36]

If Las Vegas needed the Mesquite Club, so, too, did Helen. The group provided her with a forum for spreading her ideas, a means for undertaking civic projects, and a venue for socializing with the women friends who were so important to her. The club members, for their part, revered her as a heroine. Her close friend Delphine Squires later wrote: "When we think of a pioneer woman living on a ranch in the midst of a desert area. It is quite natural to picture her as a big strapping individual with the strength to meet most any emergency that might arise such as milking a dozen cows, mending a pasture fence or ploughing a furrow or two ... but not Helen J. Stewart. She was (Dresden China) doll-like, tiny and full of femininity, with a gentle disposition. Her eyes were bright and shining and she was deeply religious, seemingly so unsuited for the role she was to play." At a May Day celebration, the members of the Mesquite unanimously chose her as the May Queen. The *Age* related: "She was escorted to a flower-laden throne and crowned with a wreath of roses."

*The Mesquite Club members in front of the house of Dr. and Mrs. Roy Martin with Helen in her usual place at the center. Nevada Historical Society*

# Chapter 8: *The Final Years*

Las Vegas women could scarcely contain their excitement over a momentous event, the arrival of Mary Belle Viley Park, the wife of dentist, Dr. William Park. Kentucky born, Mary Belle was a product of a highly refined segment of plantation society with strict rules of etiquette, such as banning the display of an uncovered female forearm before three in the afternoon. Moreover, this arrival from another world that Las Vegans had only glimpsed in the pages of fashion magazines had invited all of them to a social in her new brick house — an occasion both frightening and thrilling. The cause of their quandary was hats. A number of ladies felt they owned no hats suitable for such a gala affair. They solved this dilemma with an agreement that those wearing hats would remain at the social only a short time, as was expected, and then depart and pass along their hats to friends. Mary Belle expressed some surprise to Delphine Squires over the duplication of hats. She was even more aghast at the behavior of Helen Stewart. Instead of departing after the short interval decreed by Kentucky etiquette, Helen passed through the receiving line, commandeered a chair, and rocked there for the entire afternoon. Delphine explained to Mary Belle that during Helen's many years as mistress of the Mormon Trail, the welcome visits of guests were measured in days, not minutes. Mary Belle and Helen soon became good friends, and Mary Belle Park would be a leader in Las Vegas society for the rest of her days (no doubt with some adjustments to western life).[1]

In the new Las Vegas, Helen's lonesome days beside the trail were over. To her women friends, she must have been a delightful companion, cultivated, interested in every subject, and with no unkind word for anyone. She interacted with them on all sorts of occasions, partnered with them on civic efforts, and led in forming the clubs they enjoyed together. Foremost among these was the Mesquite Club. Elected president by the forty-five members in 1916, Helen "in her gentile manner guided the destinies" of the group during the following year, in the phrase of the *Age*. She also remained a leading charter member of St. Agnes Guild, the ladies' association of her church.[2]

Added to these were various civic activities that had included pressing for the display of Las Vegas Valley produce at the 1911 Chicago Land Show, in keeping with her long-standing belief in the importance of agriculture in a balanced community. Moreover, she was asked to take charge of the Arbor Day program in 1917, for which she was the logical choice in view of her role in planting the town's first trees. She served on the board of the local cemetery, "Woodlawn." Pleased by the board's success in beautifying the cemetery with trees, shrubs, plants, and walkways, Helen wrote Tiza that it had become so pretty that "Very few people now send their loved ones away."[3] Another step on the pathway to civilization.

Some have wondered where Helen stood on one of the burning issues of the time — woman suffrage — and whether she had contact with Nevada's best known suffragist, Anne Martin. Although Helen made no speeches and left no written statement on the subject, she obviously favored the participation of women in public life, and this issue was no exception. Martin's only link to Las Vegas, which she never visited, was a letter addressed generally to the Mesquite Club. Possibly, if Helen and Martin had

HELEN J. STEWART: FIRST LADY OF LAS VEGAS

met, they might not have liked each other much. Martin, while she deserves full credit for keeping the issue on the agenda, was more confrontational. Helen's methods, by contrast, were tactful and gentle. For example, instead of fiery speechifying about the need for women on the school board, she simply would offer herself as a candidate for election (and win).

Florence Boyer, daughter of Delphine Squires, described the advent of woman suffrage in Las Vegas in 1912. At that time, "they were rather active on the suffrage question up in Reno, but down here in Clark County, there hadn't been any great activity. That is, the women all felt that if they had told the men that they wanted the vote when it came to election time, they would give it to them if they didn't antagonize them. They didn't do too much about it." Nevada, one of the only two western states that had not accepted woman suffrage, had advanced part way through the complicated process of amending the state constitution. The 1911 legislature had voted to grant women the franchise; the 1913 legislature had not yet met, and if these lawmakers voted favorably, the popular referendum would occur in 1914.

A wire from Reno to Delphine Squires, then president of the Mesquite Club, announced that a nationally known suffragist, Mrs. Charlotte Perkins Gilman, would be arriving in Las Vegas to speak and asked them to secure a hall. Quoting Delphine, Boyer continued: "I somehow felt very uncomfortable, because I was sure she would say something that would make the men mad. However, I consoled myself with the thought that in all probability there would not be many men there." She could envisage just four, including her own husband and Frank Stewart, "all dragged there against their will by their wives." (The first sign that Helen favored suffrage.)

As the 1914 referendum approached, the Las Vegas ladies adhered to their policy of gentle persuasion and pillow talk to win over male voters. Suffrage won the referendum decisively, with 10,936 voters in favor and 7,258 opposed. The issue lost in the traditionally republican and conservative northwest, Reno and nearby counties, where Anne Martin had been most active. Among all the counties, Clark ranked second highest in the percentage of favorable votes (75.5 percent). Evidently, gentle persuasion was not an ineffective strategy.[4]

Important as her civic activities were to her, Helen was first and foremost the matriarch of a large and changing family, and some of her hopes for them would be realized. New Year's Eve 1916 was the scene of more than the usual festivities, being the occasion of Eva's wedding at Helen's home. The "good man" Helen had wished she would marry had arrived in the person of Clarence Stay, six years younger than Eva. Clarence's business was groceries, but his passion was mining, perhaps to the detriment of the Stewarts, who often invested with him. A great deal of money had been made in mining. Rumor had it that Lena's third husband, Sam Yount, had gained hundreds of thousands at Goodsprings, which bought him a very handsome Los Angeles home, different from the Pahrump abode of the old trail days when the Stewarts and the Younts had traded holiday visits. Unfortunately, Clarence's dabbling in mines did not yield similar results, although his enthusiasm remained unabated. His hobby was "petting" and humoring his cars, also enjoyed by Eva and Helen. In the Ford that he boasted could "go anywhere a donkey can climb," many conveniences became possible — and even a picnic in El Dorado Canyon. Unlike Rucker, he enjoyed a cordial relationship with his mother-in-law.[5]

The Stays lived with Helen, whose heart and home were always open to her family and friends. These included her former daughters-in-law, still part of the family in her eyes, and they warmly reciprocated her affection. All the same, Eva felt that some friends trespassed too much on Helen's hospitality. Overwhelmed with the care of her ailing one-year-old and with her second baby almost due, she wrote Tiza in exasperation. "I sure have been sick & to think the whole d — Gann family have been over and you know how lazy they are ... I am getting sick of them. They never offer to help with a thing."[6]

Despite the love and support of the Stays, Helen wrote in the summer of 1917 that I'm "getting more lonesome as I grow older." She would soon find it harder to be lonesome, as Eva's babies began arriving in quick succession, and the house rang with children's voices. First came Clarence Junior, born on April 28, 1918, when Eva was thirty-five. Although it was a difficult birth, neither mother nor baby suffered any harm. Two years later Francis arrived, "perfectly handsome" in his affectionate grandmother's eyes, and, when less than a month old, looked as though he "might be a priest or a Lawyer." Evelyn followed, and finally Clinton, when Eva was well into her forties. Clarence showed himself a devoted father, and Eva had been transformed into a complete homemaker, with none of Tiza's wanderlust (perhaps she had enough of travel during the years of following the races with Jimmy). She cooked, she baked, she gardened, she canned, she mothered her growing brood, she cared for Helen in illness, and she dearly loved her husband. Seeing them together, Helen realized that "he means so much to Eva's happiness health and general welfare."[7] Some dreams did come true.

*Will with his daughter, Helen Jane, named for his mother.*
*Nevada State Museum Las Vegas*

HELEN J. STEWART: FIRST LADY OF LAS VEGAS

For Will, Helen's hopes for a better life came to pass more slowly. When he decided to run for long-term county commissioner in 1920, Helen wrote Tiza. "I hope he will succeed as it will give new impetus in life." She later reported, "He allready has a self reliant look in his face." There is a hint in the correspondence that Will had been drinking but had recently desisted (he "is now a strictly temperate man"). It also appears that he had been subsisting in part by farming and by county jobs cast his way by friends, for instance overseeing the construction of the state highway near Searchlight and transporting some boys to the Elko reform school. Although he had many friends and his wife, Mina, electioneered for him among her relatives in the Moapa, Helen wrote anxiously: "I do hope Will will be elected as it means much in the future for him."[8]

Soon she could happily report that the voters elected Will by an overwhelming majority. "We were proud of the way his friends stood by him and glad that Will could have a chance to prove the Metal that was in him." Once more the "watchdog of the treasury" was on the job, and Clark County would undergo no embarrassments on the order of Lincoln County's notorious million dollar courthouse. Will's stewardship as chairman of the board of county commissioners was so popular with voters that at the next election for long-term commissioner four years later no other politician even bothered to oppose him.[9]

Regrettably, the watchdog was less successful in managing his own finances than those of the county. Despite his inheritance and his early holdings in Las Vegas real estate, he appeared financially strained. The reasons probably lay in unsuccessful mining investments and bad luck. In 1925, his house burned in a fire that consumed all the family's possessions, and they managed to escape with only their night clothes. For the time being, they lived in a tent. Building a new house proceeded slowly because Will had to partially depend on materials salvaged from the burned house, an indication of his limited funds. All the same, although the salary of a commissioner was small, he had a regular income, and Helen chose to consider him re-established. He had shocked her, however, with an unavoidable reminder of the passage of time. Helen wrote Tiza: "Day before yesterday was Wills birthday and I was surprised to go back over the years and find it made him fifty years, Could it be possible that fifty years had passed since that eventful morning in March 9th 1874. To be sure I am not mistaken I will stop now and go and look into the first leaves of my Bible that has been my companion and friend since childhood, and in which those most wonderful Events of my life are written down for future reference ... Sure eneough, it is true."[10] The wonderful event of that day in Pony Springs with her well-loved Archie must have seemed several lifetimes ago.

Then there was the matter of Tiza. She continued her wandering ways, and Helen, in letters overflowing with affection for her "Darling Girlie," continued her unrelenting campaign to persuade Tiza to marry and settle down in Las Vegas. In 1916, Tiza began studying medicine, of which her mother disapproved. Helen need not have worried; Tiza had taken up and put down several pursuits in the course of her travels, including selling millinery and clothing and, in Snow Ball, Arkansas, selling pianos, player pianos, and organs. Helen did not fail to add, "I will feel happier and better satisfied if I know there is some one there that loves you and will be true to you in sickness and trouble."[11]

In the summer of 1917, Helen's letter sounded a similar refrain. She hoped Tiza's "Beaux is just the one to make you happy and if he isent you better come out in Nevada and Marry some of these Rich Mining Men. They are not so young as they used to be but they are making the money." Helen added almost as an afterthought that Frank had been unwell, probably not realizing that he would never be well again. He had throat cancer. On September 1, 1918, he died and Helen wrote Tiza: "He had been suffering so long and desired to pass away from the pain that though he dreaded the approach of death and the final dissolution." Eva and Helen had exhausted themselves nursing Frank in his last days. "We were up many nights with Mr Stewart and Eva and I were so worn out and exhausted the last ten days and nights we hardly knew we slept and for two nights after he was gone we could not sleep It seemed every atom of my body had for awhile stood still and every nerve and muscle and movement of my body had become tense." Helen buried Frank in the Woodlawn Cemetery, not the family burial plot in the "Four Acres." Despite denying him this parting accolade, she apparently missed him, writing Tiza, "I would be too lonely for expression were it not for the two families here with me."[12]

Tiza occasionally visited but continued to reject a permanent return. Why did she resist? Answers are necessarily a matter of conjecture. Perhaps she simply enjoyed the liberating freedom of new places, new people, and trying on other lives. Or possibly she had needed to move out of her mother's shadow. Although Helen's ways were gentle, none would deny that she was a strong and dominant personality. Life had made her so. It is possible that Helen's offer to open a real estate office with Tiza or to take trips to California together were not the inducements that Helen supposed. On her visits, Tiza would win the hearts of several young relations. When she had departed, Helen's namesake, obviously charmed by this special aunt, went around the yard calling her. After a subsequent visit, Clarence, Jr. would race to Helen's typewriter and busily rattle the keys, saying that he was writing to Aunt Tiza; if she sent no reply, she was to be told that he would write her no more letters.[13]

*This photo of Tiza, dressed in high fashion, shows why men found her so attractive. (1909) UNLV Special Collections*

Further correspondence between Helen and Tiza followed the usual pattern. Tiza continued her travels, mainly in the Midwest, which Helen regarded as the land of cyclones, tornadoes, and "fearful cold weather" that she remembered only too well. Tiza, now in her forties and obviously a woman of great charm, continued to attract new "beaux," raising Helen's hopes that she would marry and settle down. In 1919, when Tiza mentioned a man named Joe, she urged her to bring him to Las Vegas, promising a feast of Eva's canned fruit. When Tiza took up with a minister, Helen encouragingly wrote: "It might be a good idea to have a real live Minister in the family, So go ahead sister." Tiza went ahead, to new men and new places, and Helen wrote of the latest one the following year: "If you cannot leave him bring him along. We will be good to him." Unfailingly she pled with her errant daughter to come home. Not until after her mother's death would Tiza finally divorce Rucker and settle in Las Vegas.[14]

Much about the private Helen is revealed in her letters to Tiza, carefully saved by Tiza through all her travels. However, Helen was also a public figure covered by newspapers and recognized by politicians as she pioneered in areas where women had not ventured before. In 1915 she became the first woman elected to public office in Clark County. The office, a place on the county board of education, well suited her long-standing belief in the importance of education. Re-elected to the board every two years, she would remain until she chose to step down in 1922. In the first decades of the twentieth century, this was a daring move; even in sophisticated New York, the appointment of women to the county board of education in 1909 made front page news in *The New York Times*. In 1916,

Helen took another leap forward and ran as a Republican for the State Board of Education. The Democrats also endorsed her, and she was quietly proud of winning with sixty-three percent of the vote, "elected by all my friends," as she put it. Privately, there is a sign that even before this statewide accolade she felt exuberant over her achievements and the recognition she had received. In 1915, she wrote Tiza: "Today is the day enjoy it live it and each day that follows ... wear it in your crown and the dawning of each morning will be filled with glory."[15]

Although her role on the state board is difficult to assess, her imprint on the county board stands out unmistakably. When the board planned a new high school, she was an influential member, elected clerk and continuing at the head of the board until 1921. Her part in the planning of the new high school was indirectly acknowledged when she was invited to speak and preside over the laying of the corner stone in October, 1917. The new high school ranked as a capital investment for Clark County. Some thought it larger than necessary. Not Helen, with her unwavering faith in the future of the community.[16]

An unprecedented crisis — the Spanish flu pandemic of 1918 — demanded close coordination between the county board of health, the school board, and the principals. It struck Las Vegas in mid-September when local physicians reported twelve cases. This ballooned to eighty within a week, then one hundred forty, with five more every day. The county board of health ordered all churches, theaters, and schools closed, and panic reigned. The first death occurred on October seventh. With the crisis seeming to ease, the schools re-opened on November fourth, only to be closed again by the board of education because many pupils still lay ill with flu. A month later, on December second, the schools opened and closed again, but a week later they opened and stayed open with a "fair attendance" and even a dance on the fourteenth. Although the county health officer promptly banned further dances, Las Vegas was returning to normal. Helen and all her family appear to have escaped the dread disease. Nonetheless, Helen and Eva frequently suffered from what Helen was prone to call "La Grippe," perhaps a number of garden variety flues. All the same, occasional bouts with La Grippe did not prevent Helen from participating, with characteristic energy, in activities to aid the war effort in 1917-1918. During many hours spent working for the Red Cross, she knitted bed socks and sweaters and sewed night shirts, comforters, and bed pillows. Although her presidency of the Mesquite Club had expired, she chaired a program under the auspices of the General Federation of Women's Clubs appealing to every American club woman to donate a dollar for building and maintaining furlough houses for American soldiers in France.[17]

One last time Helen was in the vanguard breaching another barrier against women. Until 1922 women had never served on Clark County juries. According to a poll, lawyers thought women unsuited to jury duty because, as one attorney put it, "they cannot give a good looking or a magnetic man a fair and impartial trial." Evidently, the killer in this murder trial, Nick Dugan, was not excessively magnetic. The ladies appeared unfazed by the unsavory aspects of the shooting, a standard drunken brawl in the ill-famed "block sixteen," a hotbed of prostitutes, gambling dens, and saloons imperfectly disguised in deference to Prohibition.[18]

Helen was described as the most active and alert juror on the panel. Her eyes never left Dugan's face as he described the night on which he consumed seventeen alcoholic drinks and finally shot a man who protested against his abusive language. Finding Dugan guilty was the only possible conclusion. The questionable part arose on the degree of his guilt — first or second degree murder or manslaughter. It took three ballots for the jury to agree. Initially, the women, in their traditional role as the civilizers of the West, censoriously voted for second degree murder, while the men on the panel voted for manslaughter, perhaps moved by the old mining camp sense of brotherhood and an awareness that "there but for the grace of God go I." On the second ballot the men persuaded two women to agree to voluntary manslaughter; on the third the remaining two women accepted the lesser charge, and the trial was over. Dugan received a light sentence of eight to ten years in prison, and Clark County women received acceptance as jurors.[19]

"Now Mrs. Stewart is a person to be reckoned with in those parts," wrote the appropriately named journalist Gordon Gassaway when recounting his tour of the highlights of southern Nevada. In fact, Helen was gaining recognition beyond "those parts." In 1915, the commissioners for the Panama-California Exposition approached her about bringing her basket collection to San Diego for the event. Unfortunately, the state of Nevada failed to appropriate enough money for the expenses, and Helen tartly observed to Tiza, "Imagine they will stay here."[20]

Helen's efforts to make the history of southern Nevada better known and to illustrate Southern Paiute culture through her baskets added to her own renown throughout

HELEN J. STEWART: FIRST LADY OF LAS VEGAS

the state. In the autumn of 1915, she served as delegate and guest of honor at the Federation of Women's Clubs conference in Yerington and read a paper on the history of southern Nevada and her time beside the Mormon Trail when the Las Vegas Valley was remote from the world. She also exhibited a few of her baskets, telling the story of how she came to possess each one and revealing in the telling much about her life among the Southern Paiutes.

*A special Paiute basket withheld from the sale and recently donated by Helen's descendents to the Nevada State Museum Las Vegas. Nevada State Museum Las Vegas*

After the conference, she visited Jeanne Wier in Reno before proceeding to Carson City, where she was the guest of Governor Emmet Boyle and his wife. On seeing her baskets, Abe Cohn, the basket connoisseur who sponsored the famed Washo basket maker, Dat-So-La-Lee, admitted that Helen's baskets were the most beautiful he had ever seen. One had fifty-two stitches to the inch, with feathers of the yellow hammer woven into the design, whereas Dat-So-La-Lee's best did not exceed thirty-two stitches per inch. Helen continued her journey to Galt for a visit with her aging mother before returning to Las Vegas. Much impressed by this pioneer icon, Governor Boyle appointed her one of the delegates to the Twelfth Annual Convention of the American Civic Association in Washington D.C. in 1916. "It is quite an Honor," Helen wrote Tiza, "and if I had plenty of money would sure go." This may have been just an excuse, or it may have been the truth.[21]

The governor had not yet abandoned his effort to honor this remarkable lady. In mid April 1918, he appointed her a delegate from Nevada at the annual meeting of the National Conference of Social Work to be held in Kansas City. Although Tiza offered inducements — she would pay her mother's railroad fare and meet her in Kansas City, where they would go shopping — Helen again declined the honor. This time for good reason. Eva was about to give birth to her first child and Frank was suffering dreadfully. Tiza thought that "surely they can get along at home without you for a while," but with Helen it was always family first.[22]

Efforts to involve Helen did not cease. In 1920, Jeanne Wier appointed her to head one of the Nevada Historical Society's Las Vegas committees, and almost at the end of her life, Governor James Scrugham appointed her to the Historical Research Committee. There is no small irony in the circumstance that Helen, who had not wanted to move to the Las Vegas Valley, had emerged as the leading authority upon its history. And what is more, had grown to love it. "I will take the Desert any day for mine," she firmly declared, taking pleasure in the multiplicity of spring wild flowers and the doves cooing in the old cottonwood.[23]

A contagious climate of optimism surrounded Helen in the early twenties. Real estate boomed, as she never failed to remind Tiza, several entrepreneurs grew rich from nearby mining, and surveyors started preparing for Boulder

Dam (later renamed Hoover Dam). Helen was not immune. She expected that the power from the great dam would furnish abundant electricity for many purposes, including pumping up ground water for farming, and the Las Vegas Valley would turn into the agricultural paradise of her vision. When setting off into the hills with Eva and Clarence in 1921, she sounded as buoyant with hopes of finding a "Big Rich Mine" as any seasoned prospector.[24]

Yet the shadows were lengthening. Following a paralytic stroke in 1915, Delia had been cared for in Galt by her daughter Rachel. The formidable frontierswoman who had crossed the plains by wagon in 1863 with infant twins at her breasts and three small children at her feet had reached the end at eighty-five in 1919, far older than the average woman of her time. Now Helen stood at the leading edge of the generations. Despite her many successes and honors, she, who had weathered such tragedies with spirit, had started to see the world more darkly. As she put it to Tiza, "The great Fever of life has burnt out." Despondent comments began to appear occasionally in her correspondence: she sometimes felt "so tired of this great confusion of existence;" she found life "rather monotonous at the best." What once gave her pleasure had ceased to do so. She noted her Mesquite Club responsibility as president was over and she was quite relieved. This attitude was unusual for the woman who had been a founding member of the Mesquite Club and St. Agnes Guild and had recently founded a new club. "I have handled and dusted and washed Indian Jugs. and cleaned and dusted untill I would like to go out in the mountains and find a Wic-i-up and stay there awhile ... Everything seems to make me so tired. I suppose one of these days I will take a notion to sail sky ward and forget it all." It was the first time that she had found the care of her treasures onerous.[25]

Helen evidently reached the nadir of depression after an unspecified quarrel with her sisters. "Some of the coals have burnt so deep that they have left scars and they have hurt in the burning." She even sorrowed for the old ranch, now long neglected and falling into rack and ruin. She wrote William Clark: "It makes me sad now when I see the Trees being destroyed and the many things that are losing their usefulness and beauty. I feel sometimes like going among them and trying to preserve them." William Clark had visited her twice that summer, once accompanied by his wife and child, and admired her basket collection. Helen wondered if he might trade the old ranch for the baskets, but Senator Clark, polite admirer though he was, would never be the man to relinquish control of property. This was the first hint that Helen might consider parting with her treasures.[26]

To the end, Helen's interest in the Indians never wavered. Although she had expressed weariness with club activities, she founded one more club in the summer of 1919, the U-Wah-Un Study Club. According to Helen, the name meant "circle of friends" in Southern Paiute. It met twice monthly; its membership was limited to twelve, including Mary Belle Park, the former Kentucky socialite; and the group was as serious as its name implied. Assigned topics for the meetings included women's issues such as the effect of woman suffrage and women in politics, but unsurprisingly, Indian issues loomed large. Helen often led the discussion on such subjects as our responsibility toward our Indians and causes for Indian discontent.[27]

During Helen's last years, the fate of her basket collection

HELEN J. STEWART: FIRST LADY OF LAS VEGAS

became an issue. In a November 17, 1918, letter to Helen, Jeanne Wier made "bold to open the question" she had never had the courage to ask: what did Helen plan to do with the baskets? And if sold, at what price? Wier of course hoped that the Nevada Historical Society might have "the honor" of housing them. Helen did not respond until June 17, 1919, explaining that "sickness and grief kill the spirit" and the deaths of her husband and mother and a severe bout of flu in her family had delayed her. Apparently, she was not yet ready to part with the baskets, because she wanted to add "a few more little things" to make the collection complete. Having no idea of the collection's worth, she named no price. Nor did she make any move to have it evaluated, although a likely expert, a visiting Columbia University professor, had much admired it and Abe Cohn, Dat-So-La-Lee's mentor, would have been a good source for an evaluation. Still, everyone interested — and probably Helen herself — thought she should be paid.[28]

She made her wishes clear, however. The basket collection was intended for "future benefit to my Home and State." She wanted to write a book on the meaning of the baskets and many Indian legends that would provide "a History of a people that has lived nearer to God and Nature than any race of people on the face of the earth." At this point Helen's letter became somewhat incoherent. "In their Basketry the Sun, Moon, Plantes, and Stars and Milky Way the Snow Rain Winds Lightening Heat and cold. The springs streams rivers valleys and mountains are all discrivedand given their work in Natures great forces the Birds of the Air. The Beasts of the fields The creeping creatures are each given a study and a lesson to the untamed nature of the Indian." She wanted the proceeds from the book donated to the Las Vegas Indian school.[29]

Money would prove to be the sticking point. Perhaps Helen naively supposed that the next legislature (1921) would appropriate an adequate sum. Jeanne Wier, wiser on the penuriousness of the legislature, knew this to be unlikely. Nonetheless, she offered no practical fundraising plan and wrote that a donation from Senator Clark was the only hope — equally unlikely, since Clark had no commitment to Nevada. Wier, of course, was obliged to deal with many necessities, including the illness of her mother, but she was no stranger to creative fundraising. In 1909, when the state completely deleted the appropriation for the Historical Society, it survived by subscriptions. With equal ingenuity, she might, for example, have approached a wealthy Nevadan with a stronger interest in the state than Clark, or engaged in broader fundraising, perhaps through the state Federation of Women's Clubs. She took no action, however.[30]

A few people floated practical plans. Mr. Chapman, a deputy superintendent of schools in Clark County, proposed that he would interview Helen on southern Nevada history and the Indians while a stenographer took down her responses. He would then develop a series of books for school children with Helen as author and himself as collaborator. The program outlined by Rita Breeze, wife of a prominent attorney and much involved in a movement to market works by women writers, envisaged several logical steps: first, an evaluation by an expert; second, a $5,000 appropriation from the legislature to buy some of the baskets; third, books to be published by the Historical Society according to Chapman's plan. The books would attract so much "notice" that at a subsequent session the legislature would fund the rest of the collection. Another proposal in December, 1920 came from Delphine Squires. She suggested that her husband, Charles, the long time editor of the *Age*, could collaborate with Helen to preserve the "valuable data that she cannot arrange herself." Delphine, a close friend of Helen's on the spot, knew just how frail Helen had become, as Wier in distant Reno did not, and Delphine feared that much of the early history of Clark County would be lost "should she be taken away." None of these ideas came to pass. Chapman received no funds for a stenographer; Squires and Helen did not collaborate. Although Helen gave some effort to compiling a Southern Paiute-English dictionary, she never started her book.[31]

An undated typescript, possibly one of the speeches she gave, offers a taste of part of the book she might have written. She began: Initially the Indians were "wild creatures." In 1882, at the Moapa Reservation in the Moapa Valley, she saw the Indians subsisting "half clothed, half fed, under the old time agency rule." However, the off-reservation Indians lived better, kindly treated by the early settlers and miners who employed them and encouraged them to cultivate the land around the smaller springs. This changed. "With the advent of the Railroad came the white homeseeker and all of the available land was soon occupied in small holdings, each one doing his own labor leaving the Indian with no land, no home, an Ishmaelite in the land he had known as his own. The white hunter also climbed the mountainsides and where had been plenty of deer and mountain sheep, there was none."

"What can be done for the Indian?" Helen rhetorically inquired. Her answer was a ringing manifesto that predictably followed her long-standing belief in education. "Provide schools for them … Teach the girls domestic science: teach the boys agriculture. Among them there are artists and musicians and literary characters. There must be some way provided for them … The time of the wild Indian has passed."[32]

Helen's health began to deteriorate. By January 1924, she realized that her illness was serious. Before leaving for Los Angeles for treatment, she executed a bill of sale in which she turned over all of her personal property, including her house and the 550 Indian baskets, to her three children for one dollar in consideration of the love and affection she bore them. This document would avoid any legal entanglements after her death, when it would be recorded. Will and her old friend Birdie Gann brought her to Los Angeles.[33]

Las Vegas was shocked to learn that Helen had cancer. While in Los Angeles, Helen was cared for by her two former daughters-in-law, Lena Yount, now married to her third husband, and Dreeme Benson, married to Dr. Samuel Benson and the mother of one more child, both women living in the Los Angeles area. Hira and Dreeme's two children were now young adults. Dreeme not only opened her home to Helen when she was released from the hospital but devoted herself to Helen's care, later writing Tiza: "Of all the people I have met, of all the ones I have known she has been the dearest the most understanding, her love and sympathy has helped me through some of the darkest hours of my life, just to know that one person loved and understood has meant more to me than any one will ever know."

When Helen needed to go to the doctor's office for

treatment, Lena and Sam Yount took her in their enclosed Nash auto, regarded as a fancy conveyance. Without "hedging," Dreeme wrote Tiza on Helen's condition. She had uterine cancer that had spread so widely that an operation was out of the question. Instead the doctor would undertake a "radium treatment," inserting a small tube of radium into the ulcer. This would not effect a cure but might retard the cancer's progress. Helen was not suffering and seemed to be responding well, able to eat and gaining a little color.[34]

In March, Helen's condition had improved so much that she wrote Tiza, "It looks as if I were going to get entirely well." She had gained almost twenty pounds, from her initial weight of about ninety. "I am waiting to have the Doctor give me final examination to see if I can enter the World and its activities." At this optimistic juncture, Lena and Sam Yount gave Helen a gala seventieth birthday party at their spacious Los Angeles home. It was a costume masquerade party for sixty guests, many of them Las Vegans who had traveled down for the event. Costumes included an Indian chief and fancy gypsy, an old lady and Jewish rabbi, a colonial dame, a Scotch lassie in kilts, a Spanish senorita, an Indian squaw, Japanese dancing girls, a flapper, and a sailor. Several had written tributes to Helen in poetry.[35]

In May, Helen felt well enough to go back to Las Vegas, though she would briefly return in June to Los Angeles for more treatment — and more exposure to modern ways. Dreeme joked that her daughter Virginia Benson had been corrupting Helen. She had taught the pioneer icon to shoot craps and might soon teach her to smoke cigarettes. In October came a surprise in the continuing drama of placing Helen's baskets, a deus ex machina in the person of Governor James Scrugham, who arrived with a team of archeologists. That Helen was always able to entertain any number of visitors in her modest sized house with Eva's family also in residence shows her talents as a hostess. The governor and the others were on their way to Lost City, the recently discovered ruin of an ancient Anasazi pueblo. (Today Lost City is more lost than ever; though all the archeologists could salvage is now displayed at the Lost City Museum south of Overton, the ruin itself melted away when the waters of Lake Mead, created by Boulder Dam, inundated it.) In the course of this visit, Scrugham saw some of Helen's baskets, and in February, 1925, he wrote informing her that the legislature might pass an act appropriating "a moderate sum" to buy her collection and place it permanently on display at the Nevada Historical Society. What was the "lowest figure" she would accept?[36] Helen replied in early March that she would be "much pleased" if the state bought and exhibited the baskets. Also they could be exhibited "under my personal supervision" at the 1926 state exhibition, planned to coincide with a forthcoming national rotary convention in Reno. Nonetheless, she still declined to set a purchase price, suggesting that the governor's experience in viewing art collections made him better able to decide their value. The governor visited again and expanded his offer. The state would pay a salary to Helen and an assistant if she came and showed her baskets at the 1926 exhibition. No doubt Scrugham hoped that some legislators who had not yet seen the baskets would view them and be sufficiently impressed to be generous with a purchase price. The governor also proposed that the state would copyright and publish her book, turning all profits over to the Las Vegas Indian school as she wished. A delighted Helen twice asked Tiza to come and help as her assistant. No reply from Tiza survives, but she did not come, possibly realizing, as the governor and Helen herself did not, that her mother was too frail for such an undertaking.[37]

*A sampling of Helen's large collection of over 550 Southern Paiute baskets. Nevada State Museum Las Vegas*

Unfortunately, none of these ideas came to pass. It was a feasible plan. Governor Scrugham had great interest in Nevada Indian history, and with his thrust behind it, purchase by the state might have been achieved in time. But for Helen it was too late. The stories and meaning of each basket died with her. Two years after her death, her children sold the collection for $12,500 to The Fred Harvey

Co. The company operated a chain of hotels along the Atchison, Topeka, and Santa Fe Railroad across the country. Herman Sweitzer, the Indian artifact buyer, handled the sale. He paid on the spot, and quickly recouped the investment by selling some of the best ones for high prices. The rest were to be sold as souvenirs through The Fred Harvey House Co. Today the Heard Museum in Phoenix, Arizona holds a small group of the baskets. The rest have disappeared into private hands, one hopes to be valued for their beauty, but one fears often to be abused by second and third generation owners unaware of their provenance. In 2009, a single basket, withheld by the family at the time of the sale, returned to Nevada. It was donated by Helen's descendants and is shown at the Nevada State Museum Las Vegas.[38]

The sale of the basket collection was an irreparable loss to the Southern Paiute people of their cultural heritage, indeed a loss to all Nevadans, past and future, a loss to the art world of many beautiful creations by artists who will now forever remain unknown, and a loss to the legacy that Helen had collected and preserved with such care.

In the summer of 1925, Helen "came very near passing over the river Stix," but with the aid of two doctors and home nursing, she rallied one last time. During what she termed "the last Chapter of the book of life," she remained interested in the activities around her and continued to wheel and deal real estate, calculating that her prime properties should not yet be sold because they would greatly increase in value after Boulder Dam was built. Nonetheless, her first concern had always been her family, and in her last days, her love and pride in them glows more brightly than ever. She wrote Tiza on the central and elemental meaning of motherhood: it gave a woman "a vocation in life. It cuts off all the fancy edges and brings us down to the real thing in life. The reproducing of our kind. And when you once decide upon the Job you have something to occupy any extra time you may find along the way."[39]

The doings and irresistible adorableness of her grandchildren abound in Helen's last letters to Tiza, the final one that survives being dated July 17, 1925. She writes of Clarence Jr. and little Helen praying over Francis when he had eaten too much green fruit, of Clarence's sterling performance in first grade, of the baby's attempts at talking, of little Helen going to school and "talking plainer every day." (The Helen J. Stewart School for children with special needs was named for this grandchild.) Hira's son Leslie and his wife, Mary, presented Helen with three great-grandchildren, a daughter, then twin boys. Not unexpectedly, Helen thought the twins "just Handsome." With the children around her, Helen thought, "Life is sweet, even at my age." The wandering Tiza at last came home to be with her mother, surely a balm to the heart. Finally, Helen's gallant spirit could no longer sustain her small cancer-riddled body and she died on March 6, 1926, just short of her seventy-third birthday. Her death certificate designated her occupation as "historian."

Helen's funeral procession on March 10 was the largest ever before seen in Las Vegas — and probably ever since. People poured in from all areas of the state to pay their last respects. Miners, prospectors, and Indians passed by her casket. Hundreds of floral arrangements, many sent from other towns at great expense, covered the casket and filled the church and her home. Las Vegas closed for the day to honor its first lady. The graveside service, attended only by the family and the pall bearers, did not take place for several days while a special vault was chipped in the solid caliche of the "Four Acres." Helen rested there, together with Archie, the husband of her youth, so violently torn from her forty-two years ago, her adored youngest son, little Archie, and Hira with Tiza's infant twins, little ones who would have altered Tiza's life, and Helen's with it, if they had lived. In common with much of humanity, Helen had her sorrows and her dark times, but what shines through is her joyful courageous spirit and her wise acceptance of the rhythms of life. After Frank's death she wrote: "For me give me life as long as the Lord sees fit. To be born is life to live to enjoy to suffer and to die."[40]

# Notes

## CHAPTER 1

1  C. P. Squires and Delphine Squires, "Las Vegas Nevada-Its Romance and History," 173 (henceforth Squires, "Helen J. Stewart"). Helen J. Stewart, "Phil. Foot. The. Outlaw" (unpublished article, Stewart Papers.) For some years the name varied — Las Vegas, simply Vegas, or Los Vegas, an effort by the post office to distinguish it from Las Vegas, New Mexico Territory; finally in 1903 the post office bowed to general usage, and Las Vegas became official. For simplicity, we have used this term throughout. *Pioche Weekly Record*, 20 Sept. 1890.

2  8th U. S. Manuscript Census of 1860; Sharleen Peck, Wiser Family Genealogy Forum; Pike Co. IL, Marriage Records, Vol. 1, 183, 16 Jan. 1853; Death Certificate of Helen J. Stewart, 10 March 1926.

3  Helen J. Stewart memoirs, Stewart Papers (henceforth HJS memoirs); On Colorado, see Smith, *Rocky Mountain Mining Camps*, 13-15, and Hollister, *Mines of Colorado*, 63-75.

4  On Kansas, see Zornow, *Kansas*, ch. 6, 159, 161; Robinson, *Kansas*, ch. 6; and Colt, *Went to Kansas*, 79; Brown Co. KS, Deed Records, Book E, 183-184, 11 Aug. 1868.

5  HJS memoirs. 9th U.S. Manuscript Census of 1870; Brown Co. KS, Deed Records, Book E, 183-184, 11 Aug. 1868; Record of Quitclaim Deeds, Book P, 108, 22 Nov. 1871.

6  HJS memoirs.

7  Ibid. On Rocky Mountain fever, see Shikes, *Rocky Mountain Medicine*, 30-31.

8  HJS memoirs. On early Nevada, see Hulse, *The Nevada Adventure: A History*, esp. chs. 6-7, and Zanjani, *Devils Will Reign*.

9   HJS memoirs.

10  On California, see Phelps, *All Hands Have Gone Downtown: Urban Places in Gold Rush County*, 123, 129, and Paul, *California Gold*, 284-86.

11  HJS memoirs.

12  HJS memoirs; Shover, *The Blockhead Factor: Marriage and the Fate of California's Daughters*, 34; Clover, *Hesperian College*, 102-103, 115; *Las Vegas Review*, 12 Mar. 1926. On changing California, see Paul, *California Gold*, 314-15, and Taniguchi, *Weaving a Different World: Women and the California Gold Rush*, 164.

13  HJS memoirs; 9th U. S. Manuscript Census of 1870; *Chronicle*, 18 May, 20 July, 3 Aug. 1872. Leisz family papers; Marian Leisz's ancestor, Hiram Scott, had also gone to Silver Mountain.

14  On the California milieu, see Shover, *Blockhead Factor*, 33-38.

15  HJS memoirs; Evelyn Moden, interview with Townley Porter, Las Vegas, 2 Feb. 1973; San Joaquin Co. CA, Marriage Records, Book 3, 281, 6 April 1873. *Sacramento Daily Union*, 11 Apr. 1873. On the Blossom home, see Tinkham, *San Joaquin County California*, 102.

16  HJS memoirs; Sumner, *A Trip to Pioche*, 1-12.

17  Day Book of Archibald and Helen J. Stewart, Jan. 1869-Aug. 1895, 15 Mar. 1869, Stewart Papers (henceforth quoted as Day Book). These are spasmodic journals, not a continuous record, with dates sometimes mixed. Cleaveland, *No Life for a Lady*, 157. Details on weather, etc. in the area are from Robert Steward, interview with Townley Porter, Pioche, 9 Nov. 1985. Those on the Lake Valley terrain are from Perryman and Skinner, *A Field Guide to Nevada Grasses*, 6, 184, and Barry L. Perryman, interview with Zanjani, Reno, 17 Nov. 2007.

18  Ulrich, *A Midwife's Tale*, esp. 12; Ulrich was writing on the eighteenth century, though these practices no doubt

continued on the frontier. Hoffert, *Childbearing on the Trans-Mississippi Frontier, 1830-1900*, esp. 278-79.

19  Carrie Townley, "Helen J. Stewart," pt. 1, 218; Hulse, A History of Lincoln County, Nevada, 1854-1919, 44, 45, 62; Sumner, "A Trip to Pioche," 12.

20  Buck, *A Yankee Trader in the Gold Rush*, 233, 242, 252; Hulse, Lincoln County, 48-49, 51-54.

21  Riley, The Female Frontier, 99; Carrie Townley, "Helen J. Stewart," pt. 1, 218; Hulse, "Lincoln County," 52-54.

22  Hulse, Lincoln County, 54-57; Buck, *Yankee Trader*, 249, 257-58. Squires, "Helen Stewart Builds Old Ranch After Mate Murdered by Desperado." *Las Vegas Sun*, 28 Oct. 1956. U. S. Work Projects Administration. *Inventory of the Church Archives in Nevada*, 25.

23  On Archie, see Roske, *Las Vegas*, 39-40. Lincoln Co. NV, *County Clerk's Records*, citizenship record of A. Stewart, 11 Sept. 1878.

24  Hulse, Lincoln County, 61-62, 73; Buck, *Yankee Trader*, 267, 269.

## CHAPTER 2

1  Paher, *Las Vegas*, 37. This book by historian Stanley Paher provides the definitive account of the Gass family in Las Vegas.

2  Paher, *Las Vegas*, 19-31, 37, 41. According to their tribal history, the Southern Paiute language differed somewhat from Northern Paiute and other Uto-Aztececan languages in the region. See Inter-Tribal Council of Nevada, *Nuwuvi: a Southern Paiute History*, 5; Lyman, *The Overland Journey from Utah to California*, 86.

3  Paher, *Las Vegas*, 43, 46, 50-52, 54.

4  Paher, *Las Vegas*, 41, 43, 50; Lyman, *Overland Journey*, 86.

5  Paher, *Las Vegas*, 37, 53, 55; Carrie Townley, "Helen J. Stewart," pt. 1, 220; Lincoln Co. NV, Commissioners' Records, Vol. 1, 339, 8 Dec. 1873 and Vol. 2, 46, 4 Mar.

1878; Deed Records, Book D, 44-45, 25 Mar. 1876. Dary notes, that in the West during the latter half of the nineteenth century high interest rates were common, see *Entrepreneurs of the Old West*, 243.

6  Carrie Townley, "Helen J. Stewart," pt. 1, 221-22; Lincoln Co. NV, Miscellaneous Records, Book C-2, 201-04, 1 June 1881; Deed Records, Book P, 163-165, 1 June 1881.

7  HJS memoirs. Squires, "Helen J. Stewart," 174; Mary Carman to Helen, 6 May 1882; *PR*, 15 Apr. 1882. Helen J. Stewart. "Phil. Foot. The. Outlaw."

8  Paher, *Las Vegas,* 23, 38-40. On the spring, see Whitely, *Young Las Vegas,* 2, 15, and Carrie B. Call diary, 24, Nov. 1886, n.p., Huntington Library; the Call diary is a rarity because women's diaries on the Mormon Trail are lacking, see Lyman, *Overland Journey From Utah to California*, 86.

9  Carrie Townley, "Helen J. Stewart," pt. 1, 224. On life at the Las Vegas ranch, see Paher, *Las Vegas*, 38. On attitudes of women missionaries, see Myers, *Westering Women and the Frontier Experience 1800-1915*, 51-52. Squires, "Helen J. Stewart," 175.

10  On Yount, see "Southern Nevada's Pioneer Women." Also see *Nevadan* 25 June 1967, 24.

11  Wilson Collection, Spring Mountain Ranch State Park; 7th U.S. Manuscript Census of 1850; National Park Service Civil War Soldier and Sailor System; Lincoln Co. NV, Mining Records, Book A, 23-25, 30, 15-16 July 1871; Book K, 208, 4 Feb. 1873. Nevada Division of State Parks, "Spring Mountain Ranch" 2; Sadovich, "Forgotten Pioneers," 25; Wilson Collection, UNLV; Nevada Manuscript Census of 1875; 10th U. S. Manuscript Census of 1880. Phelps, "All Hands Have Gone Downtown: Urban Places in Gold Rush California," 125-126.

12  10th U. S. Manuscript Census of 1880. Fredrick, Donna, "Hanging With Parish," 20-22.

13  Zanjani, *Jack Longstreet: Last of the Desert Frontiersmen*, 26-27, 113.

14 Squires, "Helen J. Stewart." 176; *Searchlight* 23 Aug. 1907.

15 *PR*, 17 June, 2 Dec. 1882; Mary Carman to Helen, 6 May 1882; Robert Stewart, interview with Townley Porter, Las Vegas, 9 Mar. 1972.

16 *PR*, 8 Sept. 1883, 17 June 1882. Helen J. Stewart, "Early Knowledge," 221.

17 Day Book, June 1884-Sept. 1887, Dec. 1890-Jan. 1892; Helen to Sawyer, 16 July 1884, copy in Day Book.

## CHAPTER 3

1 Helen to Sawyer, 16 July 1884, Day Book.

2 Ibid.

3 Ibid. In March of 1972 when the graves had to be relocated due to building on the site, Townley Porter assisted at the archeological excavation of the burials in the Stewart family graveyard, "The Four Acres," under the guidance of Dr. Sheilagh Brooks and Dr. Richard Brooks, professors at the University of Nevada Las Vegas. Florence Squires Boyer, interview with Townley Porter, Las Vegas, 14 Nov. 1971. Protestant Episcopal Church, *The Book of Common Prayer*, 241-244. Townley Porter established and organized the Archives of the Episcopal Church in Nevada in 1975, and oversaw it as Historiographer until 1995.

4 Helen to Sawyer, 16 July 1884, Day Book.

5 Ibid.; *PR*, 2 Aug. 1884. Day Book, 19 July 1884. Receipt for $15 to Helen, handwritten and signed by H. Parish, 19 July 1884, Stewart Papers.

6 "Adversity of Justice," undated, unsigned letter fragment, Stewart Papers. The penmanship appears to be Helen's; she may have intended to send it to a newspaper, but it has not yet been found in published form. Lincoln Co. NV, Justice Court, State of Nevada vs. Schyler Henry, Hank Parish and C. Kiel, Criminal Complaint, 20 July 1884.

7 Day Book, 11 July 1884; *PR*, 26 July, 2 Aug. 1884.

8 Stewart, "Early Knowledge," I, 221-22; *PR*, 26 July 1884.

9  *PR*, 26 July 1884; Day Book, 6, 9 July 1884; Helen to Sawyer, 16 July 1884, Day Book.

10 n.a., "Adversity of Justice," n.d., Stewart Papers.

11 Stewart, "Early Knowledge," I, 221-2; Squires, "Helen J. Stewart," 176-77; Day Book, 2 Jan. 1891.

12 *Angel, History of Nevada*, 341; Lincoln Co. NV, Probate Records 1884-1909, 2, 3, 6, 14 Aug. 1885. Measurements taken by Townley Porter on site. Helen to Delia Wiser, 15 Aug. 1884.

13 Stewart, "Early Knowledge," I, 221.

14 Day Book, 5, 11 July, 1884.

15 *PR*, 6 Sept. 1884, 20 Dec. 1890.

16 *Mohave County Miner*, 20 July 1884; Lincoln Co. NV, Commissioners' Records, Vol. 2, 300, 6 Oct. 1884, Helen to Delia Wiser, 15 Aug. 1884.

17 Day Book, Dec.1884; *PR*, 14 Feb. 1885; Storey Co. NV, Marriage Records, Book A, 331, 5 Nov. 1875. On Hiram Wiser, see for example, Day Book, 28 Oct. 1885 and 17 Mar. 1886.

18 *PR*, 21 Oct. 1885, 18, 23 Mar. 1889; Day Book, Dec. 1884; Lincoln Co. NV, Deed Records, Book Q, 198, 28 Sept. 1888; Probate Records 1884-1909, 2, 3, 6, 21 Aug. 1884. On Hiram Wiser, see for example, Day Book, 28 Oct. 1885, 17 Mar. 1886.

19 Lincoln Co. NV, Miscellaneous Records, Book C-2, 416-418, 14 Aug. 1885; Probate Records 1884-1909, 416-18, 14 Aug. 1885.

## Chapter 4

1 Call diary, 21-24 Nov. 1886.

2 Lincoln Co. NV, Probate Records, Archibald Stewart Probate File, Helen J. Stewart to Judge Rives, 29 Oct. 1885; Miscellaneous Matters, Book C, 419-422, 11 Jan. 1886.

3 John Townley, "Early Development of El Dorado Canyon

and Searchlight Mining Districts," esp. 17-18; Stewart, "Early Knowledge," I, 221; Day Book, 28 Apr.-2 May 1889; Paher, *Nevada Ghost Towns and Mining Towns*, 278-80.

4 Day Book, 3 Oct. 1884-23 May 1886, 8 Mar. 1890, 21 Feb. 1891; Stewart, "Early Knowledge," I, 215; Perkins, "On the Trail of a Renegade Pahute," 119-26. In a letter to Sheriff H.E. Freudenthal dated 3 Feb. 1897, B.F. Bonelli described Mouse as half Mexican; there is no confirmation of this, see the *PR*, 11 Feb. 1897.

5 Perkins, "On the Trail," 119-26. Mouse's wife is mentioned in Helen Stewart's Day Book (14 Nov. 1885) but not after he left the Stewart Ranch; possibly she had died or the couple had separated.

6 *PR*, 24 June 1897; H. [Harsha] White to Surveyor General Pratt, 23 May 1897 in the *Carson Appeal*, 2 June 1897; see also the 30 May 1897 issue; H.E Freudenthal to Reinhold Sadler 16 May 1897 and unsigned to Sadler 16 May 1897 (telegrams), J. Poujade to Sadler, 17 May 1897, Freudenthal to Sadler, 21 June 1897, all in the Nevada State Archives, Carson City.

7 *PR*, 4 Mar. 1897; *Carson Appeal*, 1, 17, 24 July 1897.

8 Perkins, "On the Trail," 119-26; *Carson Appeal*, 24 July 1897.

9 8th U.S. Manuscript Census of 1860; Ford to Helen, 17 Mar. 1895; Kelly, School Superintendent, 1875-76 report, Vol. 1.

10 9th U.S. Manuscript Census of 1870; *PR*, 17 May 1884, 13 June 1875, 16 , 23 Dec. 1882, 29 Mar, 1894; Lincoln Co. NV, Probate Records, File 1313, Book "blank," 259, Conrad Kiel will, Aug. 10, 1893; Commissioners' Records, Book 2, 39, 3 Jan. 1877; 4, 1 Oct. 1877; 195, 7 Aug. 1882; Miscellaneous Book, 186-187, 28 Oct. 1889; Ford to Helen, 17 Mar. 1895.

11 Day Book, 13 Feb. 1889, 17 Mar. 1895; D. M. Wiser to "folkes at the Vegas," 28 July 1887.

12 Helen to Ford, n.d., 1894.

13 "Report of State Superintendent of Public Instruction,"

Nevada, Appendix to Journals of the Senate and Assembly, 1893, 37, 1895, 38.

14 Helen to Ford, n.d. 1894; Ford to Helen, 17 Mar. 1895; Day Book, 21 Apr. 1889; *The Lode*, 29 Mar. 1894. Carrie Townley, "Digging Up History," 7-8.

15 Day Book, 3 Jan., 22 Aug., 3 Sept., 1 Oct. 1886; Helen to Ed Kiel, 9 May 1887, copy in Day Book.

16 *PR*, 5 May 1887, 3 Mar. 1889; Day Book, 28 Feb., 3 Mar. 1889.

17 Day Book, 4, 18, 22 Sept. 1886, 12-18 Apr. 1887. On the Bradfutes, see Day Book 1 Jan.-22 Mar. 1887 and Zanjani, *Longstreet*, 38-44. On Hiram, see Day Book, 28 Sept 1888.

18 Day Book, 15 Dec. 1885, 3 Jan., 5 Apr., 24 Aug., 18-23 Oct. 1886, 1, 10, 20 Jan., 12-14 Apr. 1887. On Ivanpah, also see Call diary, 24-25 Nov. 1886, and Paher, *Ghost Towns*, 274-76.

19 *Age*, 13 Mar. 1926, obituary of Helen J. Stewart reportedly written by her friend Delphine Squires; Stewart, "Early Knowledge," I, 215; Day Book, 24 Sept., 20 Oct. 1886. White, *It's Your Misfortune and None of My Own*, 151-152. On speculation, also see, Limerick, *The Legacy of Conquest*, 69. On women prospectors, see Zanjani, *Mine of Her Own: Women Prospectors in the American West*.

20 *PR*, 18, 23 Mar. 1886. On the Desert Land Act, see White, *It's Your Misfortune and None of My Own*, 151-152.

21 Clark Co. NV, Miscellaneous Records, Book 5, 452, 30 Apr. 1928; Lincoln Co. NV, Deed Book S, 219-221, 19 Nov. 1897.

22 Lincoln Co. NV, Deed Records, Book Q, 198, 28 Sept. 1888; D. M. Wiser to "folkes at the Vegas," 28 July 1887. On Longstreet also see Zanjani, *Longstreet*, 46.

23 Helen to Delia, 14 Sept. 1889, copy in Day Book; statement of H. Wiser, 9 Mar. 1894, Stewart Papers; Agreement between Helen J. Stewart, Hiram Wiser, and Andrew Shellard, 9 Mar. 1894, copy in Day Book; *PR*, 24 Mar. 1897.

24 Day Book, various dates. Robert Stewart, interview with Townley Porter, Las Vegas, 9 March, 1972.

25 Day Book, 19 Feb. 1889, 14 Jan. 1891; Scott Egy, interview with Townley Porter, Blue Diamond, 16 Nov. 2009.

26 Letters to Wilson in the James B. Wilson Collection, UNLV: Eleanor Clark (sister), 20 Dec. 1882; J. L. C. Wilson (nephew), 27 Dec. 1890; Jane A. Cullison (sister), 26 Sept. 1881; Jennie Clark (niece), 8 Mar. 1891; Mollie Crowell (niece), 14 Apr. 1891.

27 Helen to Tiza, 26 Oct. 1924. Robert Stewart, interview with Townley Porter, Las Vegas, 9 March, 1972. The dubious assertions that Annie Kayer died in 1878 and George Anderson in 1879 in California are in Rogers, "Spring Mountains Adobe Cabin Has a Varied Role in State's History." The James Wilson Papers contain correspondence to and from Anderson as late as 1886 and Annie is listed as Wilson's wife in the 1880 census. Some confusion exists over the names of the Wilson boys. In the 1880 census they are John (age 6) and James (age 9 mos.).

## CHAPTER 5

1 Zanjani, *Longstreet*, 64-66.

2 Carrie Townley, "Helen J. Stewart," Pt. 2, 4-5; Zanjani, *Longstreet*, 66-67.

3 Stewart, "Phil. Foot. The. Outlaw," Stewart Papers.

4 Zanjani, *Longstreet*, 66-69.

5 Ibid, 69-71.

6 Day Book, 3-4 May, 1891.

7 Marriage License of W. J. Stewart and Lena Carl, 5 Oct 1895, Stewart Papers; Evelyn Moden, interview with Townley Porter, Las Vegas, 2 Feb. 1973; *Las Vegas Age*, 26 Oct. 1907; Lincoln Co. NV, Deed Records, Book Y, 263, 13 Sept 1907; Marriage Records, Book B, 121, 5 Oct. 1895; Lena Carl, California Death Index, 1940-1997; Lena Carl to Helen, 10 Sept. 1903.

8 "Report of State Superintendent of Public Instruction," Nevada, Appendix to Journals of the Senate and Assembly,

1897, 46; *PR*, 7 Mar. 1895; Hafner, *100 Years on the Muddy*, 332; Robert Stewart, interview with Townley Porter, Las Vegas, 9 Mar. 1972; 11th U.S. Manuscript Census of 1900.

9  Lincoln Co. NV, Marriage Records, Book B, 129, 5 Dec. 1896.

10 Lincoln Co. NV, Commissioners Records, Vol. 1, 61, 11 July 1870, 281 15 Nov. 1872; Vol. 2, 265, 13 Nov. 1874; Vol. 3, 32: 4 Aug. 1890; *PR*, 30 Oct 1880; 1 Nov. 1884.

11 Helen to John B. Brady, 15 Mar. 1894, Day Book; Joseph Howerton to Townley Porter, 12 Feb. 1973.

12 Helen to Tiza, 21 June 1899; Day Book, 16 Oct. 1884, 20 Mar. 1886, 9 Mar. 1891.

13 Helen to Tiza, Eva, and Archie, 8 Dec. 1897, to children, 17 Feb. 1898.

14 Helen to Archie, n.d.; Tiza to Helen, 27 Nov. 1897; Helen to Archie, 16 Dec. 1897.

15 Helen to Archie, 16 Dec. 1897; Helen to Archie, 24 Nov. 1897; Helen to Archie, 8 Dec. 1897; Helen to Tiza, Eva, and Archie, 8 Dec. 1897; to children, 17 Feb. 1898.

16 *Los Angeles Record*, 26 Nov. 1897; Tiza to Helen, 27 Nov. 1897.

17 Archie to Tiza, 21 Sept. 1897; Helen to Tiza, Eva, and Archie, 8 Dec. 1897.

18 Helen to Tiza, Eva, and Archie, 8 Dec. 1897.

19 Lincoln Co. NV; Probate Records, Hiram Wiser Probate 21 Sept., 1909; Helen to Tiza, 21 June 1899.

20 Helen to Archie, 25 Jan. 1899.

21 *PR* , 20 July 1899; Helen to Tiza, 25 Jan. 1900; Townley Porter's observation at exhumation; Helen to Sadie George, Aug. 28 1907.

22 *LCR*, 19 Oct. 1900. On early structures at the Kiel Ranch, see the photos in Special Collections, UNLV.

23 *LCR*, 19 Oct. 1900.

24 Ibid.

25 Sheilagh T. Brooks and Richard H. Brooks, "Problems of Burial Exhumation, Historic and Forensic Aspects," 64-86. See also Sheilagh Brooks to Townley Porter, 12 Feb. 1973; the analysis by Carrie Townley in "Helen J. Stewart," pt. 2, 12-13; Robert Stewart, interview with Townley Porter, Las Vegas, 9 Mar. 1972. Jerry Curry, "He Heard the Shot," *Nevada State Journal*, 11 July 1976. Lincoln Co. NV, Probate Records, Edward B. Kiel Probate, Coroner's Jury Verdict, 13, Oct. 1900.

26 Henry Hudson Lee, interview with Townley Porter, Las Vegas, 14 Aug. 1971. On Lee's background, also see, Georgia Lewis, "Panaca's Favorite Son Comes Home," 30-31.

27 Dr. Phyllis Martin, "History of the Kiel Ranch Historic Site," *Las Vegas Review-Journal*, 14 Jan. 2000; Roske, *Las Vegas: A Desert Paradise*, 44-45. Ed Kiel had been briefly married 1889-91, but his only heirs were his siblings. Lincoln Co. NV, Probate File, Edward B. Kiel; Miscellaneous Records, Book C-2, 575-76, 9 May 1889. See for example, Helen to Mrs. George, 28 Aug. 1907, George Collection, UNLV.

28 Helen to Tiza, 21 Sept. 1897, Helen to Archie, 16 Dec. 1897, and Helen to children, 17 Feb. 1898. On Frank Stewart's background, also see Helen to Sheriff Sam Gay, 18 Nov. 1919.

29 Helen to Tiza, 21 June 1899; Death Certificate of Frank Stewart, 1 Sept. 1918; unsigned to Helen, 24 June 1901. See also Archie to Tiza, 21 Sept. 1897.

## CHAPTER 6

1 Hopkins and Evans, eds., *The First 100*, 17-19; Lamar, ed., *The American West*, 486-87.

2 Myrick, *Railroads of Nevada and Eastern California*, v. 2, 626.

3 Carrie Townley "Helen J. Stewart," pt. 2, 13; McWilliams to J. Ross Clark, 16 Jan. 1902. Unless otherwise noted, all correspondence on railroad matters is located in the Union

Pacific Railroad Collection, UNLV. This collection also contains records of the San Pedro, Los Angeles, and Salt Lake Railroad.

4   Myrick, *Railroads*, v. 2, 640-44. Also especially see, Hopkins and Evans, eds., *The First 100*, 17-19.

5   William Clark to Helen, 10 June 1906, Stewart Papers. Lincoln Co. NV, Miscellaneous Records, Book F, 237-39, 14 Oct. 1902.

6   Hopkins and Evans, eds., *The First 100*, 17-19; Lincoln Co. NV Miscellaneous Records, Book F, 237-39, 14 Oct. 1902; an undated bibliographic note with the Union Pacific Railroad Collection relates its provenance.

7   McDermott to Whittemore, 7 Nov. 1902 and to J. Ross Clark, 9, 16, 20 Nov. 1902; J. Ross Clark to McDermott, 15 Nov. 1902; undated report by McDermott.

8   McDermott to J. Ross Clark, Nov. 16, 20, 24, 1902; 31 Mar. 1903.

9   McDermott to J. Ross Clark, 16 Nov. 1902; Whittemore to William Clark, 20 Dec. 1902.

10  McDermott to J. Ross Clark, 16 Nov. 1902, with supplementary report, 8 Dec. 1902, 31 Mar. 1903; Whittemore to William Clark, 20 Dec. 1902.

11  McDermott to J. Ross Clark, 8 Dec. 1902; Robert Stewart, interview with Townley Porter, Las Vegas, 9 Mar. 1972.

12  McWilliams to J. Ross Clark, 12 Dec. 1902; McDermott to same, 24 Nov. 1902; J. Ross Clark to Whittemore, 9, 27 Dec. 1902.

13  Whittemore to William Clark, 20 Dec. 1902. On the water issue, also see George Talbot to J. Ross Clark, 14 Dec. 1902 and Helen's views in McDermott to J. Ross Clark, 15 Dec. 1902.

14  McDermott to George Holt, 29 Dec. 1902; G.E. Gibbon to Helen, 26 Feb. 1903 (telegram).

15  J.K.W. Bracken to J. Ross Clark, 9 Mar. 1903; Whittemore to same, 13 Apr. 1903; McDermott to Holt, 29 Dec. 1902;

J. Ross Clark to McDermott, 19 Dec. 1902; Helen to F. R. McNamee, 22 Jan. 1903.

16 McDermott to J. Ross Clark, 11, 19 Dec. 1902; 31 Mar. 1903. On the Kiel Ranch, see Lincoln Co. NV, Miscellaneous Records, Book F, 32-34, May 27, 1901.

17 On the Stewart departure from the ranch, see McDermott to J. Ross Clark, 31 Mar. 1903. Robert Stewart interview with Townley Porter, Las Vegas, 9 Mar. 1972.

18 Ibid. *LCR*, 26 June 1903; *The Searchlight*, 3 July 1903.

19 Ventura Co. CA, Marriages, Book 5, 223, 21 July, 1903; Clark Co. NV, Miscellaneous Records, Book 5, 405, 21 July, 1903, recorded 14 Mar. 1928. Florence Squires Boyer, interview with Carrie Townley, Las Vegas, 14 Nov, 1971; Squires, C. P., "Clark County," 797-802. "Helen J. Stewart," 177. On women's struggle for a voice in domestic financial decisions, see Prescott, "Why she didn't marry him: Love, Power, and Marital Choice on the Far Western Frontier," esp. 40-41.

20 Sacramento Co., CA, Deed Records, Book 115, 16-19, 10 June, 1884, Book 118, 436, 24 Jan. 1887, Book 132, 214, 24 Jan. 1891, Book 134, 624, 25 Mar. 1891; Book 156, 257, 8 Jan. 1896; Tax Assessors Maps, Galt, vol. 2, 64. 1898; Alameda Co., CA, Real Estate Deeds, Book A-1, 131, 20 May, 1909; F. M. Husted, Publisher, *Sacramento County Directory for 1892-1893*, p. 618; *Los Angeles Times*, 31 July, 1902 (Marriage License to John Goldsworthy); Helen to Tiza, 6 Oct. 1906; 3 Feb., 1906; 15 Apr. 1909; 12 Jan., 1914; 11 May, 1914. Boyer, *Las Vegas, Nevada: My Home for Sixty Years*.

21 Lincoln Co. NV, Deed Records, Book U, 201-203, 302-304, 2 June, 1903; *LVA*, 19 Aug. 1905. Ross W. Smith to J.K.W. Bracken, 24 June 1903; Bracken to J. Ross Clark, 19 Oct. 1903; J. Ross Clark to Bracken, 22 Oct. 1903.

22 Lena to Helen, 10 Sept. 1903. On railroad progress, see Roske, *Las Vegas*, 54-55.

# CHAPTER 7

1  Paher, *Las Vegas*, 70.

2  Paher, *Las Vegas*, 78-80; Roske, *Las Vegas*, 55-56.

3  Paher, *Las Vegas*, 87.

4  Paher, *Las Vegas*, 78-80.

5  Paher, *Las Vegas*, 87.

6  Paher, *Las Vegas*, 83; Lewis, "Las Vegas Losing Old Landmarks," 30-31.

7  Myrick, *Railroads*, v. 2, 457-61; Roske, *Las Vegas*, 59-60.

8  Roske, *Las Vegas*, 58; Myrick, *Railroads*, v. 2, 660.

9  Paher, *Las Vegas*, 91; Lewis, "Letter," 3; Moehring, "Nevada Railroad Town," 467-9.

10 Stewart, "Early Knowledge," I, 220-222; "Thirty-Two Years," *Age*, 16 Nov. 1912; Leif Whitmore, "Helen Stewart: Visionary," *Las Vegas Newspapers Real Estate*, 5 Sept. 2004, n.p.; Christ Church, Las Vegas Parish Record Book, Vol. 1, pp. 101-102.

11 William Clark to Helen, 10 June 1906; Scott, "A Thousand Miles of Desert and Mountains: a Prospecting Trip across Nevada and over the Sierras," v. 1, 25. Zanjani, *Goldfield; The Last Gold Rush on the Western Frontier,* 95, 232. On Frank's mining, see Jones, "Life Today Salutes Women's Contributions," 56. On the census, see, Paher, *Las Vegas*, 113; Moehring, "Profile of a Nevada Railroad Town: Las Vegas in 1910," 467-9.

12 Scott, "Prospecting Trip," v. 1, 27, 39; F.R. McNamee to Helen, 2 April 1911; Benjamin Goddard (L. D. S. Bureau of Information), to Helen, 11 Nov. 1908; Stewart, "Early Knowledge of Nevada," v.1, 214-22.

13 Wier, "Diary of Jeanne Elizabeth Wier," 10; Hulse, "Jeanne Elizabeth Wier's Second Career: Her 'Evolution' in History at the University of Nevada," 311-16; Squires to Helen, 19 June 1911, 27 Feb. 1915.

14 Clark Co. NV, Deeds, Book 2 , 246, 30 Dec 1911; *Age*, 6, 20

Jan. 1912, 27 Feb. 1915; *Clark County Review*, 6 Jan. 1912. Francis A. Swayne to Helen, 30 July 1912.

15 *Age*, 6 Jan. 1911, 6 , 20 Jan. 1912, 27 Feb. 1915; *Clark County Review* 27 Feb. 1915. Delay at the Bureau of Indian Affairs obliged Helen to write Senator Francis Newlands in 1915 asking him to use his influence to move the reservation along.

16 Nevada State Teacher's Certificate for Tiza Stewart, 26 Feb. 1903, Stewart Papers. Lincoln Co. NV, Book G. Misc., 176, State of Nevada, Medical Registration for Charles Augustus Rucker, M. D. 1 May 1905, recorded 23 June, 1906. *Age* 23 Dec. 1905, 9 Nov., 4 May, 22 June, 1907. Rucker to James B. Wilson (Bill), 1 Mar. 1906, Wilson Collection, UNLV. Helen to Tiza 14 Oct. 1919.

17 Townley Porter was a part of the UNLV archeology crew who were asked in 1972 to exhume the Stewart burials in the "Four Acres" to make room for a parking lot. Family members asked the crew to verify if Tiza's stillborn twins were in Hira's coffin with his embalmed remains. They were wrapped in little blankets on Hira's lap, so to speak. Although the family assumed they had been added in Las Vegas, an article in the May 2, 1908 *Age* shows this was not so. The remains of Helen, Archie, Archie Jr., Will, Hira and the twin infants were placed in Bunker's Eden Vale Memorial Park mausoleum. Megarrigle and the Indian girl, Nipe, were buried elsewhere.

18 Helen to Tiza, 8 Oct. 1908.

19 *Age*, 30 Nov. 1907, 15 Oct. 1915.

20 Helen to Tiza, 3 Feb. 1909.

21 Helen to Tiza, 15 Apr. 1909; on Helen's land dealings, see Lincoln Co. NV records and Clark Co. NV records.

22 Helen to Tiza, 6 June 1909; C.W. Wilson (Assistant Cashier, Security Savings Bank, Los Angeles) to Helen, 22 July 1909.

23 Helen to Tiza, 21 Aug. 1909.

24 Helen to Tiza, 12 Jan. 1924.

25 Helen to Tiza, 6 Oct. 1908.

26 Helen to Tiza, 3 Feb., 15 Apr., 26 June 1909; *Age,* 10 Feb. 1912.

27 Helen to Tiza, 12 Jan., 11 May 1914.

28 *Age,* 23 May, 4, 25 July 1908, 29 Oct., 12 Nov. 1910; Moering and Green, *Las Vegas: A Centennial History,* 25-27.

29 *Age,* 15 Jan., 30 July 1910, 10, 24 June, 1911, 23 Nov. 1915; Florence Squires Boyer, interview with Townley Porter, Las Vegas 14 Nov. 1971. On Will's mining, see, for example, *Age* 14 Dec. 1907.

30 On the hotel, see *Age,* 21 Sept. 1907, 30 May 1908, 26 Dec. 1908. Will quickly sold his interest to his parther. On land holdings, see the *Clark County Review,* 27 May 1911. On Los Angeles, see Helen to Eva and Jimmy, 27 Sept. 1910.

31 *Age,* 22 June, 14 Sept. 1912, 11 Jan. 1913, 11 Apr. 1914.

32 Helen to Tiza, 11 May 1914.

33 Helen to Eva and Jimmy, 27 Sept. 1910. Lincoln Co. NV, Probate Records, Hiram Wiser estate 21 Sept. 1908; *Age,* 9 Jan. 1911, 2 Feb., 3 Mar. 1912, 17 May 1913.

34 Henry Hudson Lee, interview with Townley Porter, Las Vegas, 31 Aug., 1971; Florence Squires Boyer, interview with Townley Porter, Las Vegas, 14 Nov. 1971.

35 Membership Roster, Mesquite Club Collection, UNLV; *Age,* 27 Jan. 1912; Squires, "Helen Stewart Builds Old Ranch After Mate Murdered by Desperado." *Las Vegas Sun,* 28 Oct. 1956. Legislation establishing Arbor Day in Nevada had been introduced in the legislature in 1887 by assemblyman Herman Springmeyer (Zanjani's grandfather), see *Unspiked Rail,* 28-30.

36 *Age,* 3 May 1913; Squires, "Helen J. Stewart," 173. On Helen's speeches, see for example, *Age* 10 Mar. 1911, 11 Nov. 1915.

## CHAPTER 8

1 Carrie Townley "Helen J. Stewart," pt. 2, 17; Florence

Squires Boyer, interview with Townley Porter, Las Vegas, 14 Nov. 1971. The Parks later bought the Kiel Ranch and built the large house standing there.

2  Henry Hudson Lee, interview with Townley Porter, Las Vegas, 31 Aug.1971. Mesquite Club Collection, UNLV. *Age*, 6 Nov. 1917. Christ Church, Book 1, 101-102, Episcopal Church in Nevada Archives.

3  *Age*, 4 Nov. 1911; Feb. 1917; Helen to Tiza, 1917, no specific date.

4  Boyer, "Oral History;" Howard, *The Long Campaign*, 97-98.

5  *Age*, 6 Jan. 1917. Helen to Tiza, 21 Sept. 1921; 7 Feb. 1922.

6  Eva to Tiza, Nov. 1920.

7  *Age*, 20 Nov. 1920, 6 Sept. 1924. Helen to Tiza, 17 Aug. 1917, 12 May 1918, 18 Nov., 9 Dec. 1920. Stewart Papers.

8  Helen to Tiza, 21 Feb. 1919, 12 May, 21 Oct., 9 Dec. 1920.

9  Helen to Tiza, 18 Nov. 1920; *Age*, 2 Aug. 1924.

10 Helen to Tiza, 11, 21 Mar., 27 June 1925; on mining, see for example, 2 Dec. 1916; 18 Nov. 1920.

11 Helen to Tiza, 2 Dec.1916; Tiza to Helen, 25 Apr. 1918.

12 Helen to Tiza, 17 Aug. 1917, 18 Sept. 1918; Death Certificate of Frank Royer Stewart, 1 Sept. 1918.

13 Helen to Tiza, 7 Sept. 1909, 30 Aug. 1919, 24 May; 21 Oct. 1920.

14 Helen to Tiza, 29 Jan. 1918, 30 Aug. 1919, 22, 24 May, 8 June 1920, 21 Sept. 1921. *Age*, 10 Sept. 1927.

15 *Clark County Review*, 11 Nov. 1916; Helen to Tiza, 20 Apr. 1915, 2 Dec. 1916; *New York Times*, 4 Nov. 1909. 1916 Election Results, Clark Co. NV, Election Dept. website.

16 *Age*, 6 Jan , 2 Oct. 1917. Helen was elected clerk of the board in 1917, with the understanding that the high school principal would perform the clerical duties; she continued as clerk until the 1921-22 session, Clark Co. Board of Education Minutes Book, Jan. 6 1913-Jan. 3, 1927.

17 Phillip I. Earl, "Spanish flu hit Las Vegas hard in fall of

1918," *Reno Gazette-Journal*, 13C. This comported with orders by the U.S. Surgeon General and the Nevada State Board of Health to close all schools, see *Age*, 5 Oct. 1918, *Clark County Review*, 12 Oct. 1918; also see Board of Education Minutes, 10 Oct., 4 Nov., 2 Dec. 1918. On the war effort, see Carrie Townley, "Helen J. Stewart," pt. 2, 23, *Age* 16 Mar. 1918.

18 Carrie Townley, "Bootleg, murder and women jurors," *Nevadan*, 30-31.

19 Ibid.

20 Gordon Gassaway, "Southern Nevada is Picturesque Paradise," pt. 1, g; Helen to Tiza, 20 Apr. 1915.

21 *Nevada State Journal*, 2 Nov 1915; *Age*, 9, 30 Oct. 1915; *Clark County Review*, 6 Nov. 1915. Helen to Tiza, 27 Oct. 1915, 2 Dec. 1916.

22 Helen to Tiza, 12 May 1918; Tiza to Helen, 30 Apr. 1918. Homer Mooney, Sec. to Gov. Boyle to Helen, 15 Apr. 1918.

23 Helen to Tiza, 8 June, 1920, 26 Oct. 1924. List of Nevada Historical Society committees, Wier Papers.

24 Helen to Tiza, 8 May, 21 Sept. 1921.

25 Helen to Tiza, Dec. 1917, 21 Oct. 1920, 8 May 1921. Death Certificate of Delia Wiser Goldsworthy, 16 May 1919.

26 Helen to Tiza, 31 Aug., 21 Oct. 1920, 8 May 1921; Clark to Helen, 15 Aug. 1920; Helen to Clark, 30 July 1920.

27 U-Wah-Un-Study Club Collection, UNLV. Carrie Townley, "Helen J. Stewart," pt. 2, 24-25.

28 Wier to Helen, 17 Nov. 1918; Helen to Wier, 17 June 1919.

29 Ibid.

30 Wier to Breeze, 26 July 1920; *Age*, 17 July 1909.

31 Ibid. Breeze to Wier, 20 July 1920; Squires to Wier, 5 Dec. 1920.

32 Carrie Townley, "Helen J. Stewart," pt. 2, 24-25; HJS memoirs.

33 Clark Co. NV, Miscellaneous Records, Book 5, 14 Jan. 1924.

Carrie Townley, "Helen J. Stewart," pt. 2, 24-25. Dreeme to Tiza, 18 Jan. 1924.

34 Dreeme to Tiza, 18 Jan. 1924, 5 Mar. 1926. Carrie Townley, "Helen J. Stewart," pt. 2, 24-25.

35 Helen to Tiza, 27 Mar. 1924. Seventieth Birthday Party Scrapbook, Stewart Collection, UNLV.

36 Dreeme to Tiza, 29 Jan. 1924; Helen to Tiza, 15 May, 26 Oct. 1924; Scrugham to Helen, 24 Feb.1925.

37 Scrugham to Helen, 24 Feb. 1925; Helen to Scrugham, 10 Mar. 1925; Helen to Tiza, 4 Apr., 7 May 1925.

38 Carrie Townley, "Helen J. Stewart," pt. 2, 21; *Las Vegas Sun*, 27 Mar. 2009; Paul Carson, telephone interview with Townley Porter, 14 June, 2010.

39 Helen to Tiza, 1, 27 June, 17 July 1925.

40 Helen to Tiza, 14 Oct. 1924, 11 Mar., 27 June, 17 July 1925, 18 Sept. 1918. Death Certificate of Helen J. Stewart, 26 March 1926. Carrie Townley, "Helen J. Stewart," pt. 2, 26-27.

# Bibliography

## Manuscript Materials

Call, Carrie B., Diary 21-25 Nov. 1886, Huntington Library, San Marino, California.

Carrie Townley Porter Collection, Nevada State Museum Las Vegas.

Episcopal Church in Nevada Archives, Nevada Historical Society, Reno, Nevada.

George, Hampton and Sadie Collection, Special Collections, University of Nevada Las Vegas.

Leisz Family Papers, privately held by Marian Leisz, Placerville, California.

Mesquite Club Collection, Special Collections, University of Nevada Las Vegas.

San Pedro, Los Angeles and Salt Lake Railroad Collection, Special Collections, University of Nevada Las Vegas.

Scott, Josephine Hanson. "A Thousand Miles of Desert and Mountains: a Prospecting Trip across Nevada and over the Sierras." 1914. Diary, Special Collections, Mathewson-IGT Knowledge Center, University of Nevada Reno.

Stewart, Archibald and Helen J. Collection, Nevada State Museum Las Vegas. (Items from this collection are cited as Stewart Papers.)

U-Wah-Un-Study Club Collection, Special Collections, University of Nevada Las Vegas.

Wier, Jeanne E. Collection, Nevada Historical Society, Reno, Nevada.

Wilson, James B. Collection, Special Collections, University of Nevada Las Vegas.

Wilson, James B. Collection, Spring Mountain State Park, Blue Diamond, Nevada.

# Government Records

Alameda County, California Records. Oakland, California.

Brown County, Kansas Records. Hiawatha, Kansas.

California Death Index, 1940-1997. Http://search.ancestry. com/cgi-bin/sse.dll?rank.

Clark County, Nevada Records. Las Vegas, Nevada.

Clark County, Nevada, Election Department, 1916 General Election Results, revised by Julie Ann Barker. http:/www. co.clark.nv.us/Election/Results/16_Gen.htm.

Clark County School Board Minutes, Clark County Schools, Las Vegas, Nevada.

Lincoln County, Nevada Records. Pioche, Nevada.

Pike County, Illinois Records. Pittsfield, Illinois.

Sacramento County, California Records. Sacramento, California.

San Joaquin County, California Records. Stockton, California.

Storey County, Nevada Records. Virginia City, Nevada.

State of Nevada, Bienniel Report for 1875-76, 8th session, Vol. 1, 1877.

State of Nevada, Nevada Division of State Parks. "Spring Mountain State Park," (pamphlet), 1-5.

State of Nevada, Journals of the Senate and Assembly, Appendixes, 1893 and 1895.

State of Nevada, Nevada State Archives, Carson City, Nevada.

State of Nevada Manuscript Census.

U.S. Manuscript Censuses.

U. S. National Park Service. U. S. Civil War Soldiers, 1861-1865 (database on-line) Provo, Utah. Http://search.ancestry.com.

U. S. Work Projects Administration. *Inventory of the Church Archives of Nevada,* Protestant Episcopal Church, Reno, Nevada. 1941.

Ventura County, California Records. Los Angeles, California.

# Newspapers

*Carson Appeal* (Carson City, Nevada)

*Chronicle* (Silver Mountain, California)

*Clark County Review* (Las Vegas, Nevada)

*Las Vegas Age* (Las Vegas, Nevada) abbreviated as *Age*

*Las Vegas Review-Journal* (Las Vegas, Nevada)

*Las Vegas Sun* (Las Vegas, Nevada)

*Lincoln County Record* (Pioche, Nevada) abbreviated as *LCR*

*Los Angeles Record* (Los Angeles, California)

*Los Angeles Times* (Los Angeles, California)

*Mohave County Miner* (Kingman, Arizona)

*Nevada State Journal* (Carson City, Nevada)

*New York Times* (New York, New York)

*Pioche Record* (sometimes *Pioche Weekly Record*) (Pioche, Nevada) abbreviated as *PR*

*Reno Gazette-Journal* (Reno, Nevada)

*Sacramento Daily Union* (Sacramento, California)

*San Francisco Chronicle* (San Francisco, California)

*The Searchlight* (Searchlight, Nevada)

*The Lode* (Delamar, Nevada)

# Oral Histories and Interviews

Boyer, Florence M. "Las Vegas, Nevada: My Home for Sixty Years." Interview by Mary Ellen Glass, Oral History Dept., University of Nevada Reno. 1967.

Boyer, Florence Squires, interview with Townley Porter, Las Vegas, Nevada, 14 Nov. 1971.

Carson, Paul, telephone interview with Townley Porter, 14 June, 2010.

Egy, Scott, Park Interpreter II, interview with Townley Porter,

Spring Mountain Ranch State Park, Blue Diamond, Nevada, 8 Nov. 2006.

Lee, Henry Hudson, interview with Townley Porter, Las Vegas, Nevada, 31 Aug. 1971.

Moden, Evelyn, interview with Townley Porter, Las Vegas, Nevada, 2 Feb. 1973.

Perryman, Barry L., interview with Zanjani, Reno, Nevada, 17 Nov. 2007.

Steward, Robert, interview with Townley Porter, Pioche, Nevada, 9 Nov. 1985.

Stewart, Robert, interview with Townley Porter, Las Vegas, Nevada, 9 Mar. 1972.

Squires, C. P. and Delphine Squires, "Las Vegas Nevada-Its Romance and History." Interview by Mary Ellen Glass, Oral History Dept., University of Nevada Reno. 1973.

## Books and Articles

Angel, Myron. *History of Nevada*. Oakland: Thompson and West, 1881.

Brooks, Sheilagh T. and Richard H. "Problems of Burial Exhumation, Historic and Forensic Aspects," in *Human Identification*, ed. by Ted A. Rathbun and Jane E. Buikstra, 64-86. Springfield: Charles C. Thomas, 1984.

Buck, Franklin A. *A Yankee Trader in the Gold Rush*. Letters compiled by Katherine A. White. Boston: Houghton Mifflin, 1930.

Cleaveland, Agnes M. *No Life for a Lady*. Lincoln: University of Nebraska Press, 1941.

Clover, Haworth A. *Hesperian College 1861-1896*. Burlingame: Hesperia Press, 1974.

Colt, Miriam. *Went to Kansas*. Ann Arbor: University Microfilms, 1966.

Curry, Jim. "He Heard the Shot, Grabbed His Gun, and Ran

Toward His Own Death." *Nevada State Journal*, 11 July 1976, 3.

Dary, David. *Entrepreneurs of the Old West*. Lincoln: University of Nebraska Press, 1986.

Earl, Phillip I. "Spanish flu hit Las Vegas hard in fall of '18." *Reno Gazette-Journal*, 31 Dec. 1983, 13 C.

Foster-Harris. *The Look of the Old West*. New York: Viking Press, 1955.

Fredrick, Donna "Hanging With Parish." *Nevada Magazine*, Sept./Oct. 2001, 20-22.

Gassaway, Gordon. "Southern Nevada Is Picturesque Paradise." pt. 1, *Las Vegas Age*, 2 Mar. 1918.

Hafner, Arabelle Lee, ed. *100 Years on the Muddy*. Utah: Art City Publishing, 1967.

Hoffert, Sylvia D. "Childbearing on the Trans-Mississippi Frontier, 1830-1900." *Western Historical Quarterly*, Vol. 22 (Aug. 1991) 272-88.

Hollister, Ovando J. *Mines of Colorado*. New York: Promontary Press, 1974.

Hopkins, A.D. and Evans, K.J., eds. *The First 100*. Las Vegas: Huntington Press, 1999.

Howard, Ann Bail. *The Long Campaign*. Reno: University of Nevada Press, 1985.

Hulse, James W. "Jeanne Elizabeth Wier's Second Career: Her 'Evolution' in History at the University of Nevada." *Nevada Historical Society Quarterly*, Vol. 51 (Winter 2008) 311-15.

_____. "A History of Lincoln County, Nevada-1854-1919." Masters Thesis, University of Nevada Reno, 1958."

_____. *The Nevada Adventure: A History*. Reno: University of Nevada Press, 1963.

Husted, F. M., Publisher, *Sacramento County Directory for 1892-1893*. Sacramento: F. M. Husted, 1893.

Inter-Tribal Council of Nevada, *Nuwuvi: A Southern Paiute History*. Sparks: Inter-Tribal Council of Nevada: 1976.

Jones, Florence Lee. "Life Today Salutes Women's Contributions." *Las Vegas Review-Journal*, 29 Feb. 1976, 56.

Lamar, Howard R. *The American West*. New York: Thomas Y. Crowell, 1977.

Lewis, Georgia. "Las Vegas Losing Old Landmarks," *Nevadan*, Sept., 1969; 30-31.

_____. "A letter brought the ladies back," *Nevadan*, 5 July, 1970; 3.

_____. "Panaca's Favorite Son Comes Home," *Nevadan*, 23 Mar. 1973; 30.

Limerick, Patricia Nelson. *The Legacy of Conquest*. New York: W.W. Norton and Company, 1987.

Lyman, Edward Leo. *The Overland Journey from Utah to California*. Reno: University of Nevada Press, 2004.

Martin, Dr. Phyllis. "History of the Kiel Ranch Historic Site," *Las Vegas Review-Journal*, 14 Jan. 2000 (previously published in the Western Heritage Festival & Cowboy Poetry Gathering, held November 5-7, 1999), n.p.

Melzer, Richard. *Fred Harvey Houses of the Southwest*. Charleston: Acadia, 2008.

Moehring, Eugene P. "Profile of a Nevada Railroad Town: Las Vegas in 1910." *Nevada Historical Society Quarterly*. Vol. 34, (Winter 1991) 466-487.

Moehring, Eugene P. and Green, Michael S. *Las Vegas: A Centennial History*. Reno: University of Nevada Press, 2005.

Myres, Sandra. *Westering Women and the Frontier Experience 1800-1915*. Albuquerque: University of New Mexico Press, 1982.

Myrick, David F. *Railroads of Nevada and Eastern California*. 2 Vols. Berkeley: Howell-North Books, 1962-1963.

N. A. "Southern Nevada's Pioneer Women," reprint from the *Beatty-Bullfrog Miner*, 11 Nov. 1905 in *Southern Nevada Times* 4 Mar. 1989.

Paher, Stanley W. *Las Vegas: As It Began — As It Grew*. Las Vegas: Nevada Publications, 1971.

_____. *Nevada Ghost Towns and Mining Camps*. Berkeley: Howell-North Books, 1970.

Paul, Rodman W. *California Gold*. Lincoln: University of Nebraska Press, 1947.

Peck, Sharleen, Wiser Family Genealogy Forum. Http://genforum.genealogy.comcgi-bin/pageloadgi?Hiram,Wiser.

Perkins, Geo. E. "On the Trail of a Renegade Pahute." *Nevada Historical Society Quarterly*. Vol. I, no. 3, (Winter 1958) 119-26.

Perryman, Barry L. and Quentin D. Skinner. *A Field Guide to Nevada Grasses*. Lander, Wyoming: Indigenous Rangeland Management Press, 2007.

Phelps, Robert. "'All Hands Have Gone Downtown': Urban Places in Gold Rush California." In *Rooted in Barbarous Soil: People, Culture and Community in Gold Rush California,* ed. Kevin Starr and Richard J. Orsi. Berkeley: University of California Press, 2000.

Prescott, Cynthia Culver. "'Why she didn't marry him: Love, Power, and Marital Choice on the Far Western Frontier." *Western Historical Quarterly*, Vol. 38 (Spring, 2007): 25-45.

Protestant Episcopal Church in the United States. *The Book of Common Prayer*, Oxford, England: Oxford University Press, 1867.

Riley, Glenda. *The Female Frontier*. Lawrence: University Press of Kansas, 1988.

Robinson, Sara T.L. *Kansas*. Reprint. Freeport, N.Y.: Books for Libraries Press, 1971.

Rogers, Keith. "Spring Mountains Adobe Cabin Has a Varied Role in State's History." Reprinted from the *Las Vegas Review-Journal* in the *Reno Gazette Journal*, 4 Nov. 2000, 8C.

Roske, Ralph J. *Las Vegas: A Desert Paradise*. Tulsa: Continental Heritage Press, 1986.

Roske, Ralph and Michael S. Green "Octavius Decatur Gass," *Journal of Arizona History*, Vol. 29 (Winter 1988): 371-390.

Sadovich, Maryellen V. "Forgotten Pioneers of Vegas Valley." *Nevadan*, 25 June 1967, 25.

Shikes, Robert H. *Rocky Mountain Medicine.* Boulder: Johnson Books, 1986.

Shover, Michele. "The Blockhead Factor: Marriage and the Fate of California's Daughters." *The Californians*, Sept./ Oct., 1989: 32-48.

Smith, Duane A. *Rocky Mountains Mining Camps: The Urban Frontier.* Bloomington: Indiana University Press, 1967.

N. A. "Southern Nevada's Pioneer Women," reprint from the *Beatty-Bullfrog Miner*, 11 Nov. 1905, in *Southern Nevada Times*, 4 Mar. 1989.

Squires, C. P. "Clark County," in *History of Nevada*, ed. Sam P. Davis, Vol. 2. Reno: Elms, 1913: 795-805.

Squires, Delphine. "Helen Stewart Builds Old Ranch After Mate Murdered by Desperado." *Las Vegas Sun*, 28 Oct. 1956.

Squires, Harry. "Helen Wiser Stewart — Nevada Pioneer." *The West*, July, 1969: 38-39, 63-66.

Stewart, Helen J. "Early Knowledge of Nevada," in *History of Nevada*, ed. Sam P. Davis, Vol. 1. Reno: Elms, 1913: 214-22.

_____. "Thirty-Two Years at Las Vegas," *Las Vegas Age*, 16 Nov. 1912.

Sumner, Charles A., "A Trip to Pioche," speech delivered in San Francisco, 17 Aug. 1873, Nevada State Library, Carson City.

Taniguchi, Nancy J. "Weaving a Different World: Women and the California Gold Rush." In *Rooted in Barbarous Soil: People, Culture and Community in Gold Rush California*, edited by Kevin Starr and Richard J. Orsi, 144-68. Berkeley and Los Angeles: University of California Press, 2000.

Tinkham, George A. *History of San Joaquin County California*. Los Angeles: Historic Record Company, 1923.

Townley, Carrie Miller. "Bootleg, murder and women jurors." *Nevadan*, 23 September, 1973, 30-31.

Townley, Carrie Miller. "Digging Up History," speech delivered to University Women's Caucus Forum in Reno, Nevada, 6 Apr. 1976, Carrie Townley Porter Collection, Nevada State Museum Las Vegas.

Townley, Carrie Miller. "Helen J. Stewart: First Lady of Las Vegas." Pts. 1-2. *Nevada Historical Society Quarterly,* Vol. 11-12. (Winter 1973-Spring 1974): 214-244, 2-32.

Townley, John M. "Early Development of El Dorado Canyon and Searchlight Mining Districts." *Nevada Historical Society Quarterly,* Vol. XI (Spring, 1968): 4-25.

Ulrich, Laurel T. *A Midwife's Tale.* New York: Vintage Books, 1990.

White, Richard. *It's Your Misfortune and None of My Own.* Norman: University of Oklahoma Press, 1991.

Whitely, Joan Burkhart. *Young Las Vegas.* Las Vegas: Stephens Press, 2005.

Wier, Jeanne E. "Diary of Jeanne Elizabeth Wier." *Nevada Historical Society Quarterly*, Vol. 4, (Jan.-Mar. 1961): 10.

Whitmore, Leif. "Helen Stewart: Visionary," *Las Vegas Real Estate*, 5 Sept. 2004, n.p.

Zanjani, Sally. *Goldfield; The Last Gold Rush on the Western Frontier.* Athens, Ohio: Swallow Press, 1992.

_____. *Jack Longstreet: Last of the Desert Frontiersmen.* Las Vegas: Nevada Publications, 1988.

_____. *Mine of Her Own, Women Prospectors in the American West 1850-1950.* Lincoln, Nebraska: University of Nebraska Press, 1997.

_____. *The Unspiked Rail: Memoir of a Nevada Rebel.* Reno: University of Nevada Press, 1981.

Zornow, William Frank. *Kansas.* Norman: University of Oklahoma Press, 1957.

# Index

131

Frazier, Mr.   52–54

Fred Harvey Company   169–170

Freudenthal, H. E. (Sheriff)   73

## G

Galt   19–22, 63, 97, 117, 141, 159–161

Gann, Demonia   91

Gann, Dreeme "Demi"   91

Gann, Prairie Bird "Birdie"   166

Gassaway, Gordon (journalist)   158

Gass, Mary Virgnia Simpson   38, 42, 46

Gass, Octavius Decatur   35–40, 126

Gay, Sam (Sheriff)   130

George, Hampton   103

George, Sadie   103

Gilman, Charlotte Perkins   147

Goldfield   106, 119, 122, 125, 128

Goldsworthy, John   117

Gray, Harry (Reverend)   124

Green, Dr. Sheldon   102

Green, Michael S.   38

## H

Hagerty, George   39

Hanson, El Mina "Mina"   140–141, 151

Harriman, Edward   105

Helen J. Stewart School   171

Henry, Schyler   51, 55, 58–59

Hesperian College   20–21

Hira *See* Hiram Stewart

Historical Research Committee   160

Howell, John   46

Hulse, James (historian)   29

## I

Ivanpah   38, 46, 79

## J

Jimmy *See* Coffey, James "Jimmy"

## K

Kiel, Conrad   47, 52, 53–61, 75, 98, 103, 114

Kiel, Ed   57–58, 77–78

  death of   98–103

Kiel, William   98, 100

HELEN J. STEWART: FIRST LADY OF LAS VEGAS